Of Mind and Man

The Historical Context of René Descartes'
Contribution to
Physiological Psychology

Of Mind and Man: The Historical Context of René Descartes' Contribution to Physiological Psychology

Gadfly Publishing, LLC ■ Dalton, Georgia

Publisher's Cataloging-in-Publication data

Names: Ellis, C. Arthur, author.
Title: Of Mind and Man: The Historical Context of René Descartes' Contribution to Physiological Psychology / C. Arthur Ellis, Jr., PhD.
Description: Includes bibliographical references. | Dalton, GA: Gadfly Publishing, LLC, 2020.
Identifiers: LCCN: 2020935271 | ISBN: 978-0-9820940-8-2
Subjects: LCSH Descartes, René, 1596-1650--Knowledge--Psychophysiology. | Descartes, René, 1596-1650--Influence. | Mind and body--History--17th century. | Psychophysiology--History--17th century. | Philosophy of mind--History--17th century. | BISAC HISTORY / Civilization | PHILOSOPHY / Mind & Body | PSYCHOLOGY / Physiological
Classification: LCC B1878.M55.E45 2020 | DDC 128/.2--dc23

Printed and bound in the U.S.A.

Of Mind and Man

The Historical Context of René Descartes'
Contribution to
Physiological Psychology

C. Arthur Ellis, Jr., PhD

Gadfly Publishing, LLC
Dalton, Georgia
www.gadflypublishing.com

"Changing the world, one book at a time."™

CONTENTS

BACKGROUND

The original version of this work was published in 1982 as a dissertation in partial fulfillment of the requirements for my PhD in Humanities at Florida State University. At that time, I found that the scholarly literature on Descartes primarily addressed his philosophical and mathematical works.

Since Descartes' exploration of the structure and function of the human body was largely ignored in literature, most of my research was done through written correspondence with various libraries in Europe, as well as with the renowned historian, T. S. Hall, who translated Descartes' *Treatise of Man* and published it with added commentary. After months of communication with him, I became the proud owner of an autographed copy of his work.

Since there was no internet, no cell phone messaging, and personal computers topped out at about 64K of RAM in the early 1980s, being a student at a major university with faculty members having contacts with other universities throughout the world was a great advantage. So was having an outstanding Chair of my dissertation committee, Dr. David Darst, whose constant support and encouragement made my research possible.

As a nod to history, references and works cited in this book were typewritten in 1982 (with inserted symbols drawn by hand) and have been scanned into the current publication without alteration.

PREVIOUS RESEARCH

When I decided to publish this book, part of the process was to revisit my research from the 1980s and compare it with what I could find on Amazon and other online bookstores. To my surprise, there is still no book on this topic as of this publication. Through the miracle of the internet, however, many of the sources that I used decades ago are now posted for everyone to see—if they know the keywords to search.

The primary reason for historians continuing to disregard Descartes' medical research is that his model, his analogue of the human mind and body, is no longer useful for exploring the mechanics of either, since new paradigms have evolved following his work.

Yet, a survey of the literature on Descartes' contribution to the advancement of medical science yields conflicting opinions over time.

Gregor Sebba's 1964 bibliography of works citing Descartes, covering the period of 1700 to 1960, lists only a single essay by Georges-Berthier that is relevant to the current study.[1] Sebba cites the 1745 writings of La Mettrie, who maintained that Descartes, "...blazed new trails on which, however, he then went astray."[2]

The respected early physiologist, Claude Bernard, wrote in 1872 that Descartes' work was a "physiology of fancy, almost entirely imagined."[3] On the other hand, Lemoine, writing in 1862, stated that Descartes, "...founded biology, by first explaining life in a scientific, naturalistic way."[4]

Georges-Berthier concluded that the biological research of Descartes, while philosophically sound, was scientifically unsuccessful, since his philosophy advocated a single method for all of science, including biology, but his actual findings in the sciences were not accepted by later researchers.

In 1874, T. H. Huxley acclaimed Descartes, "...a great and original physiologist; inasmuch as he did for the physiology of motion and sensation that which Harvey had done for the circulation of the blood, and opened up that road to the mechanical theory of these processes, which has been followed by all his successors."[5]

After Foster's ten *Lectures on the History of Physiology during the Sixteenth, Seventeenth and Eighteenth Centuries* was published in 1901, it became a major authoritative source for students of the history of physiology as well as for scholarly articles. Foster set the tone for future consideration of Descartes' work by stating, "Descartes was a philosopher, not a physiologist."[6]

In his dissertation for his doctorate in medical science in 1902, Auguste Tellier discussed Descartes' work as a physician and as a physiologist. While his dissertation had little influence on the academic world, he noted that Descartes was the first to explain physiological processes as purely physical forces as opposed to earlier accounts of vague and undefined "vital forces."[7]

In 1930, Franklin Fearing's book, *Reflex Action: A Study in the History of Physiological Psychology*, acknowledges the work of Descartes as demonstrating "that bodily motions might be explained without reference to a 'soul' or other nonmaterial cause."[8] In *Descartes' Traité de l'Homme*, Fearing found a "statement of how the body might carry on its functions if it were a machine constructed according to the laws of mechanics."[9]

Aside from non-psychistic explanations of animal motion, Fearing noted that Descartes was the first to make a "descriptive statement of involuntary action which bears a recognizable resemblance to the modern concept of reflex action."[10] Fearing maintains that, "The application of the principles of the 'new' physics and mechanics to the problems of muscle and nerve mark the beginnings of physiological psychology in the modern sense."[11]

Fearing summarizes Descartes' contribution to physiological psychology, stating:

> With the example of Galileo before him, Descartes had every reason to be extremely cautious in dealing with those topics on which the Mother Church might be expected to be sensitive. He described how the animal body might behave if it were a machine acting in accordance with the known laws of physics and mechanics. In man he retained the soul which through the mediation of the animal spirits could influence and be influenced by the body. He observed, however, that many of the adjustmental activities of the human body could be carried on independently of the soul.
>
> The recognition of the importance of these automatic activities and the principle of reflex action, together with the concept of animal action as dependent upon and explainable in terms of the laws of physical mechanisms, constitute Descartes' major contributions to physiological psychology.[12]

Following Fearing's study of Descartes' contribution to physiological psychology, little but passing reference was made to Descartes' biological writings until 1959, when A. C. Crombie, writing in *Scientific American*, drew attention to Descartes' achievements in this area, with special emphasis on his discovery of the adjustment of the lens of the eye.[13]

More recently, G. A. Lindeboom's *Descartes and Medicine*, revived much of the earlier work of Tellier (which, notably, was not referenced by Lindeboom).

Thomas S. Hall's 1972 translation of Descartes' *Treatise of Man* is the only translation of that work, and the introduction to this edition is the best running commentary on Descartes medical research.[14] Hall is also the author of *Ideas of Life and Matter*, a valuable text covering the history of physiology from a conceptual standpoint, and placing Descartes' achievements in historical perspective.[15]

Hall follows the lead of K. E. Rothschuh in this regard, since Rothschuh published a German version of a history of physiology (now available in an English translation by Guenter B. Risse) in 1953, which documents Descartes' role in the history of physiological thought.[16]

The first open break with Foster's 1901 *Lectures* dismissing Descartes' contributions to physiology came with Theodore M. Brown's article in the 1977 *Bulletin of the History of Medicine* in which he stated that Foster "would be rightly chided for his insensitivity to proper intellectual context and his disrespect for older but historically legitimate standards of scientific explanation."[17] In regard to Descartes' work in particular, Brown maintains, "enough evidence has already accumulated to suggest that the Cartesian mechanical philosophy was a major, and perhaps even *the* major, influence on the course of physiological development in England in this period [mid-seventeenth century]. Italy quite possibly showed similar trends."[18]

Brown further notes that three scholars—Thomas S. Hall, Gustav Scherz, and Luigi Belloni—"have begun to pay serious attention to Descartes' radically new, mechanical world view and its immediate, positive influence on his own and his contemporaries' physiology."[19]

Of the three scholars noted, Hall is the only one to directly acknowledge Descartes' role in the history of physiological psychology. Hall's statement in this regard is, "Descartes gave a special cast to the mind-body problem and largely laid down the lines along which physiological psychology, and psychology in general, were thereafter developed and debated."[20]

The fact that the value of Descartes' theories have met with mixed reviews over the centuries does not mean that they were not pioneering, and even necessary for many subsequent advancements in medical physiology.

As a case in point, incandescent lighting seems primitive when compared to LED lighting, yet no one would take credit away from Edison for inventing the light bulb. The same goes for Edison's recording cylinders compared with contemporary MP3 recordings.

More so, the laws of quantum mechanics that were held sacred during Einstein's time are now being modified as new studies probe this model's assumptions.

In each case, earlier inventions and models pave the way for new paradigms that replace the old.

The current study continues the exploration of Descartes' contribution to physiology in general, setting it within historical context, while placing special emphasis on his contribution to physiological psychology.

Notes to Previous Research

[1] A. Georges-Berthier, "Le Mécanisme Cartésien, et la physiologie au 17e siècle," Isis, 2 (1914), 37-89; 3 (1920), 21-58. Gregor Sebba's Bibliographia Cartesiana (The Hague: Nijhoff, 1964) also lists H. Dreyfus-Le Foyer's "Les conceptions médicales de Descartes," in the Revue de métaphysique et de morale, (1937), 237-286, P. Mesnard's "L'Esprit de la physiologie cartésienne," in Archives de philosophie, 13 (1937), 181-220, and the longer monograph of B. de Saint-Germain, Descartes considéré comme physiologiste et comme médecin (Paris: Masson, 1869) which is reportorial and not particularly helpful in studying Descartes' physiology.

[2] J. O. de LaMettrie, "Histoire naturelle de l'âme," first publication The Hague, 1745, Oevres philosophiques (Ambsterdam, 1753), 1, 24; see also the translation by C. G. Bussey, et al., of extracts only, published with Man a Machine . . . (Chicago: Open Court, 1912), p. 158.

[3] Claude Bernard, Leçons de pathologie expérimentale . . . (Paris: Bailliere, 1872), p. 481.

[4] [Jacques] Albert [Felix] Lemoine, L'Âme et le corps: études de philosophie morale et naturelle (Paris: Didier, 1862), p. 206.

[5] T. H. Huxley's "On the Hypothesis that Animals Are Automata" first appeared in the Fortnightly Review, Vol. 16 (1874), 555-580. The statement quoted in the text is from a reprint of Huxley's article in Significant Contributions to the History of Psychology (Series E, Physiological Psychology), Vol. IV, 556.

[6] Lectures on the History of Physiology During the Sixteenth, Seventeenth and Eighteenth Centuries (Cambridge: Cambridge University Press, 1901), p. 266.

[7] Auguste Tellier, Descartes et la Médecine, ou Relations de René Descartes avec les Médecins de son temps suivi d'un exposé des idées médicales de Descartes (Paris: L'Ecole de Médecine, 1928), pp. 43-44. This work is available from the National Library of Medicine in Washington, D.C. in microfilm format.

[8] Franklin Fearing, Reflex Action: A Study in the History of Physiological Psychology (Baltimore: Williams and Wilkins, 1930), p. 15. See also, "René Descartes: A Study in the History of Reflex Action," Psychological Review, 36 (1929), 375-388.

[9] Fearing, p. 21.

[10] Fearing, p. 26.

[11] Fearing, p. 18.

[12] Fearing, p. 28.

[13] A. C. Crombie, "Descartes," in Scientific American, 201, No. 4 (1959), 160-173. For a more detailed account of Descartes' work in optics, see A. C. Crombie, "The Mechanistic Hypothesis and the Scientific Study of Vision: Some Optical Ideas as a Background to the Invention of the Microscope," in Historical Aspects of Microscopy, ed. S. Bradbury and G. L'E. Turner (Cambridge: W. Heffer & Sons, 1967), pp. 3-112.

[14] G. A. Lindeboom, Descartes and Medicine (Amsterdam: Rodopi, 1979); René Descartes, Treatise of Man, trans. Thomas S. Hall (Cambridge: Harvard University Press, 1972).

[15] Ideas of Life and Matter: Studies in the History of General Physiology, 600 B.C.-1900 A.D., 2 vols. (Chicago: University of Chicago Press, 1969). See also Hall's History of General Physiology, 2 vols. (Chicago: University of Chicago Press, 1969).

[16] K. E. Rothschuh, History of Physiology, trans. and ed. Guenter B. Risse (New York: Robert E. Krieger, 1973).

[17] Theodore M. Brown, "Physiology and the Mechanical Philosophy in Mid-Seventeenth Century England," Bulletin of the History of Medicine, 51, No. 1 (1977), 25. Brown is also the author of an excellent thumbnail sketch of Descartes' physiology in a larger article, "Descartes," appearing in the Dictionary of Scientific Biography, ed. Charles C. Gillespie (New York: Charles Scribner's Sons, 1971), IV, 61-65.

[18] Brown, "Physiology and the Mechanical Philosophy in Mid-Seventeenth Century England," p. 26.

[19] Brown, p. 26.

[20] Thomas S. Hall, "Descartes' Physiological Method," p. 56.

INTRODUCTION

The brain is the organ through which we live, move, and have our being, a fact so elegantly expressed by Descartes in his declaration, "Cogito ergo sum."

The brain's billions of connections control the capacities of intellect, memory, emotion, self-awareness—to name just a few—representing the culmination of millions of years of evolution. Our civilizations, our cultural achievements in art and music, our subtle variations in languages, our complex technologies—all reflect the complexity of our brains.

For thousands of years human beings have tried to understand why they act, think, and feel the way they do. Using current technology, we scan brains to understand the minds of sociopaths, homosexuals, Democrats and Republicans. No group of individuals is excluded from brain scans to understand why they are the way they are.

Yet, over the course of history, the role of the brain has frequently been misunderstood, or even totally ignored. The ancient Egyptians, for example, while carefully preserving other organs in canopic jars when they mummified their dead, simply withdrew the brain in pieces through the nostrils and disposed of the remains.

Aristotle was among the earliest to assign a physiological role to the brain, teaching that its purpose was to cool the body from the excess heat generated by the heart. With the work of the Alexandrian physicians and Galen, however, many of the functions of the brain were properly attributed to it, but this knowledge was lost to the West during the Middle Ages.

In the Renaissance, Galen's work resurfaced, curiously comingled with Aristotelian and Platonic theories, and bearing little resemblance to the original work.

The failure of early philosophers and physicians to accurately determine the role of the brain is not surprising, since its physical appearance—much like 3½ pounds of custard—is rather unimpressive. Furthermore, a substantial portion of the brain, the ventricles, is filled with a fluid, which perhaps led to some early speculation that the brain served as a storage place for phlegm. Anyone with a bad head cold today can easily understand how this speculation seemed reasonable in its time.

Today, the human brain is acknowledged to be the most complex piece of matter known to man—far more complex than the most elaborate computer ever built. Its complexity is seen in its estimated ten billion neurons, each of which have tens of thousands of synapses. Attempts to design computers capable of creating artificial intelligence to imitate the functions of the human brain have led to much information about the brain's behavior but have also posed just as many problems which defy the best efforts of computer scientists.

For example, researchers once believed that the memories are stored in the brain somewhat like data is stored in a computer; i.e. certain units, or "engrams", were thought to record memories in lasting patterns of electrical circuits. Also, just as a computer stores each bit of information in its memory bank, it was assumed that the human brain stored each memory in a specific location. Clinical evidence in support of this theory includes experiments in which electrical stimulation of certain brain areas successfully evokes vivid memories in patients.

But recent research over the past several decades has demonstrated that damaging or removing portions of the brains of patients suffering from tumors or other brain disorders will diminish, but not entirely erase, memories. Consequently, the computer model of memory has been replaced by a holography model, since holograms bear a striking similarity to the brain's method of storing memories. Specifically, a small fragment of a deliberately shattered hologram will produce a complete, though blurred, image of the original recording.

While the employment of models such as computers and holograms as aids in the scientific investigation of the brain is a relatively recent development, the employment of models in the broader study of physiology dates back to Empedocles who, in the fifth century B.C., conceived of the process of breathing as a set of tubes throughout the body and posited that these function in the manner of a *klepsydra*, a kind of water clock.

The beginnings of physiological psychology, as the study of the physical basis of mind, may also be traced to ancient times, with the work of Democritus, who first attempted to reduce activities of the mind to the actions of physical forces, and to the work of Hippocrates, who suggested that epilepsy, then known as the "Sacred Disease," had a physical, not a spiritual, origin.

But the study of the physical basis of mind was lost to the West with the rise of Christianity, when the question of the seat of the soul and its "faculties"—the undefined means by which the soul interacted with the human body and its functions—become paramount to Medieval philosophers, whose work was more philological than physiological. Mental disorders, for example, were viewed as possession by evil spirits rather than any physical aberration of the brain.

It was not until the Renaissance, with the new interest in observation and the rise of anatomy as a practical science, that the speculations of the ancients were revisited. But the development of physiology in the Renaissance was slower than advances in anatomy; primarily because anatomy was a matter of direct observation of the structure of human body parts, whereas physiology required a new paradigm, a new philosophy, to create an understanding of the functioning of the human body.

This new paradigm was furnished by the advocates of mechanization at Padua and other centers of learning where the functions of the human body were frequently compared to a smoothly running clock. Descartes, and subsequently Hobbes, maintained that the body, and even the mind of man itself, was nothing more than a delicately designed clockwork.

But it was Descartes who first suggested that the functioning of the brain could be duplicated by machines, an analogy that seems less strange when one considers that the elaborately designed mechanical inventions of the 17th century were in their day regarded with as much wonder as computers are in the 20th century.

The purpose of this study is to investigate Descartes' contribution to physiology, and to physiological psychology in particular, limited to a consideration of his substitution of *physical* for *psychical* causes of sensation and lower-level cognitive functions.

This study begins with a survey of Renaissance "faculty psychology" which preceded Descartes, and continues with Descartes' ensuing development of a mechanical analogue of man, which made possible the transition from *psychistic* to *non-psychistic* investigation of the human mind.

CHAPTER 1:
THE RISE OF RENAISSANCE PSYCHOLOGY

The eminent historian of science, George Sarton, summarizes over thirty years of his studies of Medieval and Renaissance medicine by stating, "The medical Renaissance was essentially philological (not clinical or physiological)."[1] By philological, Sarton is referring to the speculative superimposition of Christian theological principles upon earlier, primarily Galenic, anatomical observations. The outcome of this model of the human mind is referred to as "faculty psychology."

Galen's work influenced the work of all physicians up to and including those practicing during the Renaissance when the English physician, William Harvey, studied it and conceived of how blood circulates in the body. As with Harvey, Descartes was familiar with the work of Galen, and incorporated some of it into his *Treatise of Man*.

Galenic Physiology

The Galenic notion of faculties, upon which later Christian philosophy was superimposed, had its origin in Galen's unique synthesis of earlier Platonic and Aristotelian philosophies, into which he incorporated the anatomical findings of the two great Alexandrians, Herophilus and Erasistratus, to form a system of physiology which prevailed in various forms well into the 17th century.

To begin with, Galen accepted the ancient Empedoclean doctrine, transmitted by Aristotle and Hippocrates, of the four "elements" (earth, air, fire, and water), embodying the four "qualities" (hot, cold, dry, and wet), which correspond to the four "essential humors" of the body (blood, black bile, yellow bile and phlegm).[2] Galen attributed health to the proper blending, or temperament, of these four elements, qualities, and humors, just as he attributed disease to their improper mingling.

The second doctrine which Galen accepted in his physiology is the Platonic Idea of the three "souls," ruling, and yet serving, the body.[3] The three souls that he described are the "rational," "irrascible," and "concupiscible," which he located in the brain, heart, and liver respectively. He maintained that the rational soul presides over reasoning and thought and provides sensation and motion; the irrascible soul controls the passions (emotions); and the concupiscible (also known as the vegetative soul) is responsible for nutrition. While he regarded the various souls as different phases or divisions of the primary soul responsible for the life of the body, Galen confessed that he was quite ignorant of the ultimate nature of the soul.[4]

In general, Galen restricted the use of the word "soul" to sentience and locomotion in animals, qualities which distinguish them from plants. In Book I of *On the Natural Faculties*, for example, Galen states:

> Since feeling and voluntary motion are peculiar to animals, whilst growth and nutrition are common to plants as well, we may look on the former as effects of the soul, and the latter as effects of the nature.[5]

As such, Galen's definition of soul would correspond to the function of the neuromuscular and sensory aspect of neurological systems in animals.[6]

The third doctrine which Galen incorporated into his physiology ls a modified version of Erasistratus' theory of pneumatology, a theory known today only from the references Galen himself makes to it. The pneumatic philosophy is based on the belief that three "pneumas" or "spirits" serve as instruments of Nature. The primary source of the pneuma present in living bodies is inspired air.

Galen's particular version of the pneumatic philosophy maintains that the flesh of the lungs processes the inspired air to becoming pneuma.[7] This subtler product is able to pass easily through the branches of the pulmonary vein, where it then passes successively through increasing refinements into the heart, liver, and brain. The final part of the process, and a concept unique to Galen, is the theory of the *rete mirabile,* or marvelous network of blood vessels he believed to be located at the base of the brain, and to which he attributes the ultimate refinement of the pneuma to form the psychic pneuma characteristic of the brain.

In addition to the various pneuma assigned to the triadic soul and its characteristic organs, Galen endows each division of the soul with a special "power" or "faculty."[8] Thus the brain has the "psychic" faculty, the heart has the "vital" faculty, and the liver has the "natural" faculty. But, in the case of the faculties, Galen goes further in stating that not only the three ruling viscera but also most of the other parts of the body have their own unique faculties.

For example, all parts of the body have an "attractive" faculty (the ability to attract from the blood the nutrients appropriate to them), a "retentive" faculty (the ability to hold this nutrient until the full benefit is received from it), and an "expulsive" faculty (the ability to rid itself of the excess or residual matter).

Aside from the foregoing, Galen makes use of faculties to the point of absurdity: the arteries have a "pulsative faculty," the muscles a "contractile" faculty, the veins a "hematopoietic" faculty, and so forth. In short, whenever an action is necessary, there appears to be a faculty created by Nature to accomplish it.

Even more mysterious is Galen's belief that faculties may occur separate and apart from the part of the body that possesses them, so that there is an overall "sympathy" or union of various parts of the body to achieve the common good.[9]

Yet, Galen's use of faculties to explain bodily functions becomes clear when he admits that so long as we are ignorant of the true essence of the cause which is operating, he calls it a faculty.[10] In this respect, the notion of "faculty" serves as a kind of black box, a place keeper to insert the results of future research.

The last element of Galen's physiology, the notion of "innate heat," reflects the Influence of Hippocrates and Aristotle. Galen rejects the opinion of Erasistratus, Praxagoras, Philotimus, Asclepiades, "and innumerable others," that the heat of the body is not innate but acquired from without.[11] Instead, he maintains that the heat of the body is not only innate but that it is somehow closely associated with the soul and is seated in the heart and arteries.

The foregoing are the general principles upon which Galen's physiology ls founded.

The basic ideas of Galen's system may be seen in Figure 1 and expressed as follows: [12]

1. Food, traversing the alimentary tract, is absorbed as chyle, collected by mesenteric vessels, and passed from them through the portal vein to the liver. There it is elaborated into venous blood and imbued with "natural spirit," a substance that is present in all living things. Charged with the natural spirit, venous blood is distributed throughout the body by the actively contracting liver. Since the natural spirit is eventually absorbed by the body, there is no need for a circulatory system.

2. A portion of the natural spirit trickles through [imaginary] pores in the septum of the left ventricle of the heart. There it meets air that comes by way of the venous artery (pulmonary vein) from the lung and the outer world. The pneuma of the inspired air acting on the natural spirit, converts it to a higher form, the vital spirit, which is distributed to the organs by the aorta and its branches.

Some of the vital spirit ascends to the brain through the carotids. These, upon entering the cranial cavity, divide into tiny vessels, the mirabile, at the level of the pituitary. The mirabile [actually not found in man] is the site where vital spirit is transformed into animal spirit [also called psychic spirit]. This flows through the nerves (which are assumed to be hollow as the blood vessels are hollow) to various parts of the body, and is responsible for both motor and sensory nervous activity.

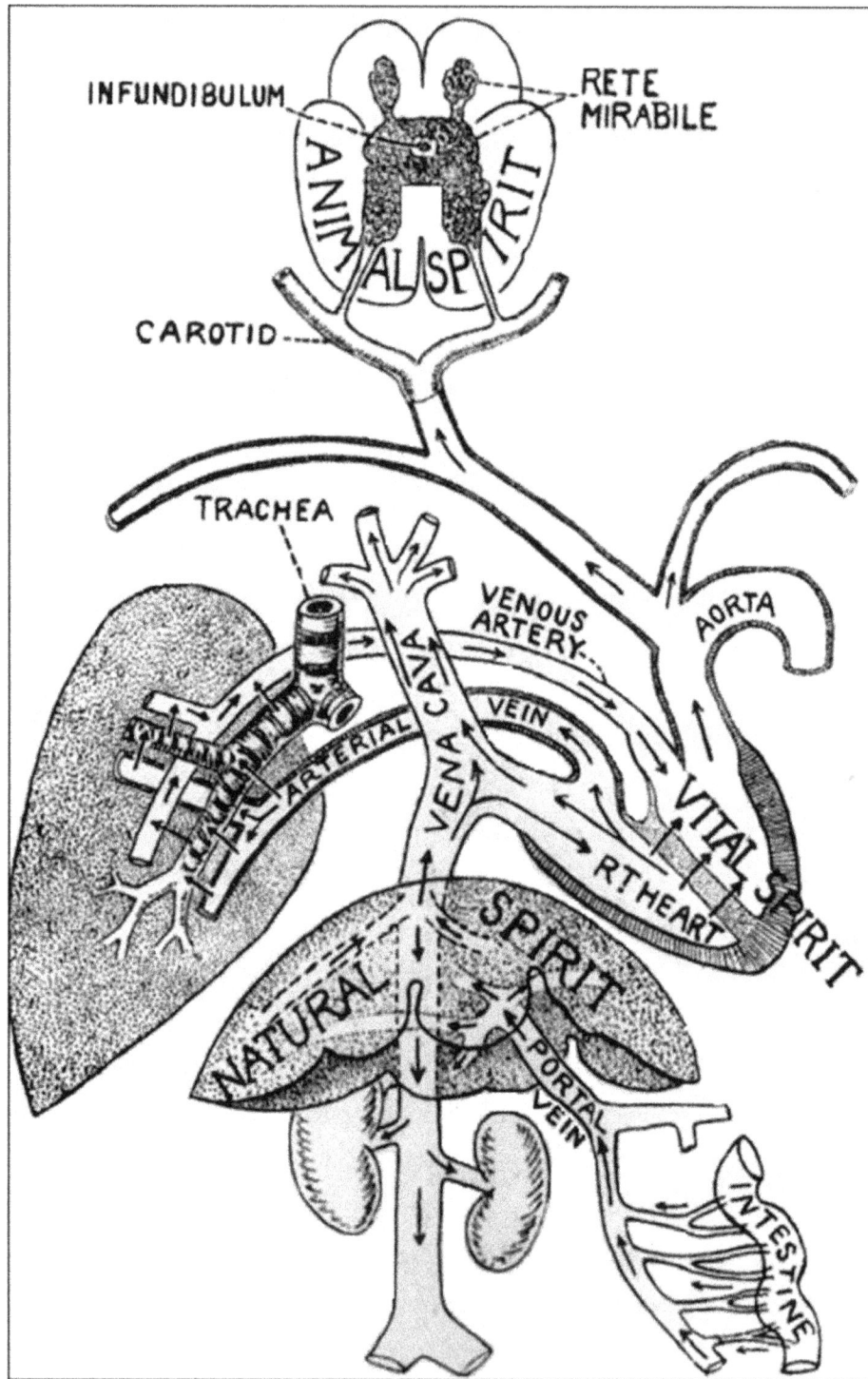

Figure 1.

Galen's Physiological System

Galen's Conception of the Psychic Faculties

To the contemporary reader, the localization of cognitive functions in the brain is accepted without objection; but for Galen, establishing the brain as the point of origin of the nerves—and, therefore, of control over the various senses—was a matter of observation and proof, since Aristotle had maintained that the primary purpose of the brain is to offset the heating effect of the heart:

> Others who hold this doctrine are less to be wondered at, but it is impossible not to be altogether amazed at Aristotle, who does not neglect the things to be seen in dissection, who is not untrained in their usefulness, who says himself that some questions require solution, others correction, and still others the testimony of the senses, and who yet is found distrusting his sense perceptions and unmindful of himself. For the encephalon is always discovered to be warmer to the touch than the air around us, but Aristotle says it was formed to cool the heat of the heart, and he forgets that he himself has said that respiration takes place for the sake of cooling; it is right, however, to praise him when, following Hippocrates, he gives a true account of the usefulness of respiration.[13]

Not only did Aristotle maintain that the function of the brain is to moderate the heat of the heart, but he also denied that all of the nerves of the senses originate in the brain. Galen is incredulous at Aristotle's lack of observation of this anatomical fact:

> "But," says he [Aristotle], "not all the instruments of the senses extend to the encephalon." Aristotle! What a thing for you to say! For my part, I am certainly ashamed even now to mention the subject. Does not a nerve [n. vestibulococh- learis] of considerable size along with the membranes themselves enter each ear? Does not a portion of the encephalon much larger than that proceeding to the ears come to each side of the nose? Do not one soft nerve [n. optlcus] and one hard one come to each eye, the former inserted into its root and the latter into the muscles moving it? Are there not four nerves extending to the tongue, two [n. lingual is from the mandibular division of the trlgeminal] of them soft, that reach it by way of the palate, and two [n. hypoglossus] hard, that descend beside the ears? Hence all the Instruments of the senses—if we are to believe our eyes that see and our hands that touch them—communicate with the encephalon.[14]

Aside from anatomical observation, Galen employed vivisection experiments on unspecified animals to test local brain function:

> Should the dissection be thus performed, then after you have laid open the brain, and divested it of the dura mater, you can first of all press down upon the brain on each one of its four ventricles, and observe what derangements have afflicted the animal. I will describe to you what is always to be seen when you make this dissection, and also before it, where the skull has been perforated, as soon as one presses upon the brain with the instrument which the ancients call "the protector of the dura mater." Should the brain be compressed on both the two anterior ventricles, then the degree of stupor which overcomes the animal is slight. Should it be compressed on the middle ventricle, then the stupor of the animal is heavier. And when one presses down upon that ventricle which is found in the part of the brain lying at the nape of the neck, then the animal falls into a very heavy and pronounced stupor. This is what happens also when you cut into the cerebral ventricles, except that If you cut into these ventricles, the animal does not revert to its natural condition as it does when you press upon them. Nevertheless, it does sometimes do this if the incision should become united. This return to the normal condition follows more easily and more quickly should the incision be made upon the two anterior ventricles. But if the incision encounters the middle ventricle, then the return to the normal comes to pass less easily and speedily. And if the incision should have been imposed upon the fourth, that is, the posterior ventricle, then the animal seldom returns to its natural condition.[15]

As to the location of the soul, and thus of psychological activity, Galen prefers the brain substance itself:

> As for me, arguing in accordance with the evidence revealed by dissection, it seems to be acceptable that the soul itself resides in the body of the brain where it produces reasoning, and the memory of sensible images is preserved there.[16]

Regarding the subdivisions of the soul within the brain, Galen favors a tripartite plan:

> Thus the sensitive soul has five distinct functions; seeing, smelling, tasting, hearing, and touching. The motor soul has one closely related Instrument and one kind of

movement, as has been demonstrated in the book, *On Movement of Muscles*, but it has various special Instruments so that it may seem to have various forms. The remaining function of the soul, which arises from the principal [mental] faculty is divided into imagination, reason, and memory.[17]

In the same chapter, Galen discusses mental disturbances, and argues that each of the faculties of the mind—imagination, reason and memory—could be affected separately. From this, Galen infers a localization of function in the brain, but does not commit himself to exact sites:

Therefore let us examine the injuries of the principal [mental] functions, and first of the imagination. Injury of this is also like another paralysis which is called torpor and catalepsy, just as another injury, distorted and wandering movement, which is called delirium; another deficient and weakened movement, as in coma and lethargy. Nay more, a kind of paralysis of function, madness; that which is like deficient movement of it, stupidity and folly; and that which is like aberration is called delirium. For very often delirium is found in both at the same time, in distorted imagination and inept reason; however, sometimes it is only in one of them, Just as occurred in the case of the sick physician Theophilus who, although he otherwise conversed sagaciously and recognized those present, believed that there were pipers in the corner of the house where he was lying, and that they continually played their pipes, producing music; he believed that he observed some of them standing, others sitting, continually piping day and night, so that he cried out, constantly ordering them to be ejected from his home. Later, after he had convalesced and recovered from this kind of delirium, he told everything which each visitor had said and done, and he remembered the appearance of the pipers. To some there ls no appearance of a vision [hallucinations], but when the reasoning faculty of the soul has been affected, they are afflicted with frenzy, as occurred to one who, when the doors had been bolted, threw vessels through the windows; afterwards he asked a passerby to order him to throw things, and clearly gave the names of the different vessels; in this manner he obviously demonstrated that he was injured neither in the imagination nor in the memory of names. Why then did he wish to throw down and smash everything? He was unable to understand this, but through his activity he indicated his delirium. As regards the memorative faculty of the soul, the symptoms appear not only in those who are ill, but also in those who escape illness; this may be learned from Thucydides who declares that some preserved from a pestilence so far forgot all that had preceded as not only to forget their own households but even themselves.[18]

Nemesius and the Early Ventricular Localization of the Faculties

Because those who followed Galen were generally inclined to accept his opinions without question, it is of considerable interest to note that the localization of mental phenomena proposed by Galen was not followed implicitly. While Galen had correctly favored a localization of mental faculties within the brain substance, an erroneous deviation in favor of the ventricles of the brain occurred, and the Aristotelian faculties of the *sensus communis*—along with imagination, reason, and memory—were located in the lateral, third, and fourth ventricles respectively.

The first surviving elaboration of the ventricular localization of the psychic faculties is contained in *On Human Nature* by Nemesius, Bishop of Emesa, in Syria.

Little is known about the life of Nemesius, except that he was an early Christian philosopher who probably wrote his single work in the last decade of the fourth century.[19] In his *On Human Nature*, Nemesius attempts to interpret Greek scientific knowledge of the human body from the standpoint of Christian philosophy, and his writings were held in high regard by both Albertus Magnus and Thomas Aquinas.[20]

Nemesius discusses the form and function of the brain, based primarily on Galenic sources, but he places the mental faculties in the ventricles, not the substance, of the brain and so elaborates the ventricular or cell doctrine of the faculties which will dominate medical writings until the seventeenth century.

While Galen praised Nature as designing the body of man and animals with perfect harmony between structure and function, Nemesius, a Christian philosopher, begins his treatise with a discussion of the nature of the relationship between soul and body. After considering the opinions of the great philosophers who came before him, Nemesius reaches his own conclusion:

> There is, in fact, general consent that the soul deserves more regard than the body, and that, indeed, the body ls only an instrument employed by the soul. The truth of this is proved by death. For, when death severs soul from body, the body lies completely still and passive, just like a workman's tools after he has gone away and left them lying.[21]

As the instrument of the soul, Nemesius maintains that the body is constructed to serve the soul as a servant does his master:

> Now the body, as being the soul's instrument, has its various parts allotted to different faculties of the soul. For the body is well and aptly furnished to serve these faculties, lest any faculty of the soul should find the body a hindrance. For to each faculty of the soul there has been allotted its own portion of the body to be its means of action, as this book will show, as it proceeds.[22]

After establishing the nature of the body/soul relationship, Nemesius turns to the localization of the faculties of the soul within the bodily structures:

> Now, as organs, the faculty of imagination has, first, the front lobes of the brain and the psychic spirit contained in them, then the nerves impregnated with psychic spirit that proceed from them, and, finally, the whole construction of the sense- organs. These organs of sense are five in number, but perception is one, and is an attribute of the soul. By means of the sense-organs, and their power of feeling, the soul takes knowledge of what goes on in them.[23]
>
> ....
>
> So, then, the faculty of imagination hands on to the faculty of intellect things that the senses have perceived, while the faculty of intellect (or discursive reason) receives them, passes judgement on them, and hands them on to the faculty of memory.
>
> The organ of this faculty is the hinder part of the brain (called also cerebellum and hinder-brain} and the vital spirit there contained. Now, if we make this assertion that the senses have their sources and roots in the front ventricles of the brain, that those of the faculty of intellect are in the middle part of the brain, and that those of the faculty of memory are in the hinder brain, we are bound to offer demonstration that this is how these things work, lest we should appear to credit such an assertion without rational grounds. The most convincing proof is that derived from studying the activities of the various parts of the braln.[24]

The justification for localizing the faculties in the ventricles of the brain offered by Nemesius in the ensuing pages of his work is based upon Galen's observations of abnormal behavior following injury to selected portions of the brain, but Nemesius departs from Galen's decision to locate the faculties in the liquid filled ventricles of the regions described rather than in the solid substance.

Overall, Galenic physiology was highly appealing to Nemesius as an early Christian, incorporating as it did elements of Stoicism and Platonism. But Galen's primary goal, to relate structure with function, was not shared by Nemesius, whose aim as a Christian philosopher was to seek an intermediary between body and non-corporeal soul. The Galenic notion of pneuma or spirits suited Nemesius' needs, but Galen's choice of brain substance as the seat of the rational soul was less desirable than the "pneumatic" spaces of the ventricles which contained the purified "psychic spirit."

Medieval Forms of Ventricular Localization

It was Nemeslus' choice of the ventricles of the brain as the seat of the various "faculties" of the rational soul which prevailed throughout the Middle Ages. The ventricular or cell doctrine as set forth by Nemesius was, however, the simplest form of the theory, which then became further elaborated and subjected to complicated rearrangements, depending primarily upon which translator or commentator revised the work.

Since *On Human Nature* left the hands of its author, its fate has been to suffer cycles of oblivion and rediscovery:

1. The first period of oblivion followed the decline of the Antiochene school after the secession of the Nestorians, of whlch Nemesius was a member.

2. The work was rediscovered in the first half of the eighth century by John Damascene, a priest from Jerusalem, whose writings incorporating the work of Nemesius became one of the classics of Greek orthodoxy.

3. In the ninth century, the Nestorlan Timothy I, under Harun al Raschid, in response to Muslin interest in the learning of the Greeks, became a patron of translators from Greek into Syriac. Nemesius' work was thereby translated and passed into the Muslin world.

4. In the tenth century, a monk and physician called Malerius, from the monastery of the Holy Trinity in the neighborhood of Tiberiopolis in North Phrygia, translated the work.

5. In the eleventh century, Nicholus Alfanus, a Greek scholar and humanist, came to Salerno from Monte Cassino to be abbot of the San Benito monastery and afterwards to be archbishop there. Alfanus made a Latin rendering of Nemeslus under the title *Premnon Phystcon* (*Key to Nature*), without reference to its original title or author. His version of Nemesius' work was known to Albertus Magnus.

6. Toward the end of the eleventh century, Richard Burgundto, Professor of Law at the University of Pisa, produced a Latin version of Nemesius from the Greek text. Burgundto's version of Nemesius' work, along with translations of some of Galen's work, were known to Peter Lombard and Thomas Aquinas.

7. Numerous subsequent editions of Nemesius' work were published throughout Europe in the Renaissance and thereafter: Venice (1400's), Strassburg (1512), Nuremberg (1500's), Leyden (1636), Basel (1562), Antwerp {1565), Parts (1638), London (1636), and Oxford (1671).[25]

Nemesius' *On Human Nature* enjoyed wide distribution throughout the Middle Ages and into the Renaissance. Much intriguing speculation based upon the account of the ventricular system of the brain, which was universal in the Medieval West and East, resulted in numerous examples, both in manuscripts and in early printed books, of the way various authors illustrated their accounts of it.[26] Two examples, one from Avicenna and one from Albertus Magnus, will serve to illustrate the major differences between Christian and Muslim versions of the doctrine.

Figure 2 is from Albertus Magnus' *Philosophia Naturalis*, a work dealing with the nature of the soul and the body in man.[27] This particular plate is reproduced from the 1490 edition, and contains the usual functions allocated to the ventricles of the brain with the exception of the inclusion of "membro Motiva" in the third cell (the fourth ventricle).

Figure 3 is from a Latin translation of Avicenna's *De generatlone embryonls*, copied ca. 1347.[28] The only legend is the statement, "This is the anatomy of the head for physlclans." The five senses are Indicated, and there are five (cf. Magnus' three) ventricles, each of which is interconnected.

The most Important development in Avicenna's theory of brain function was the addition of a dynamic element to the original static model of Nemesius.[29] A sequence of events, sometimes compared to the process of digestion, was thought to take place within the brain, starting in the first cell and ending in the third, thus accounting for the dynamic nature of mental functions. Consequently, the images created by the sensations in the first cell were processed in the second cell (reasoning), and certain portions were then stored in the third cell (memory).

Aside from Avicenna's description of the ventricular theory of brain function in his *De generatione embryonis*, a relatively minor work, there is a similar description in his *Canon*, the influence of which rivaled the writings of Aristotle and Galen in the Middle Ages and beyond. In Book I of the *Canon*, Avicenna gave additional commentary on his theory of brain function:

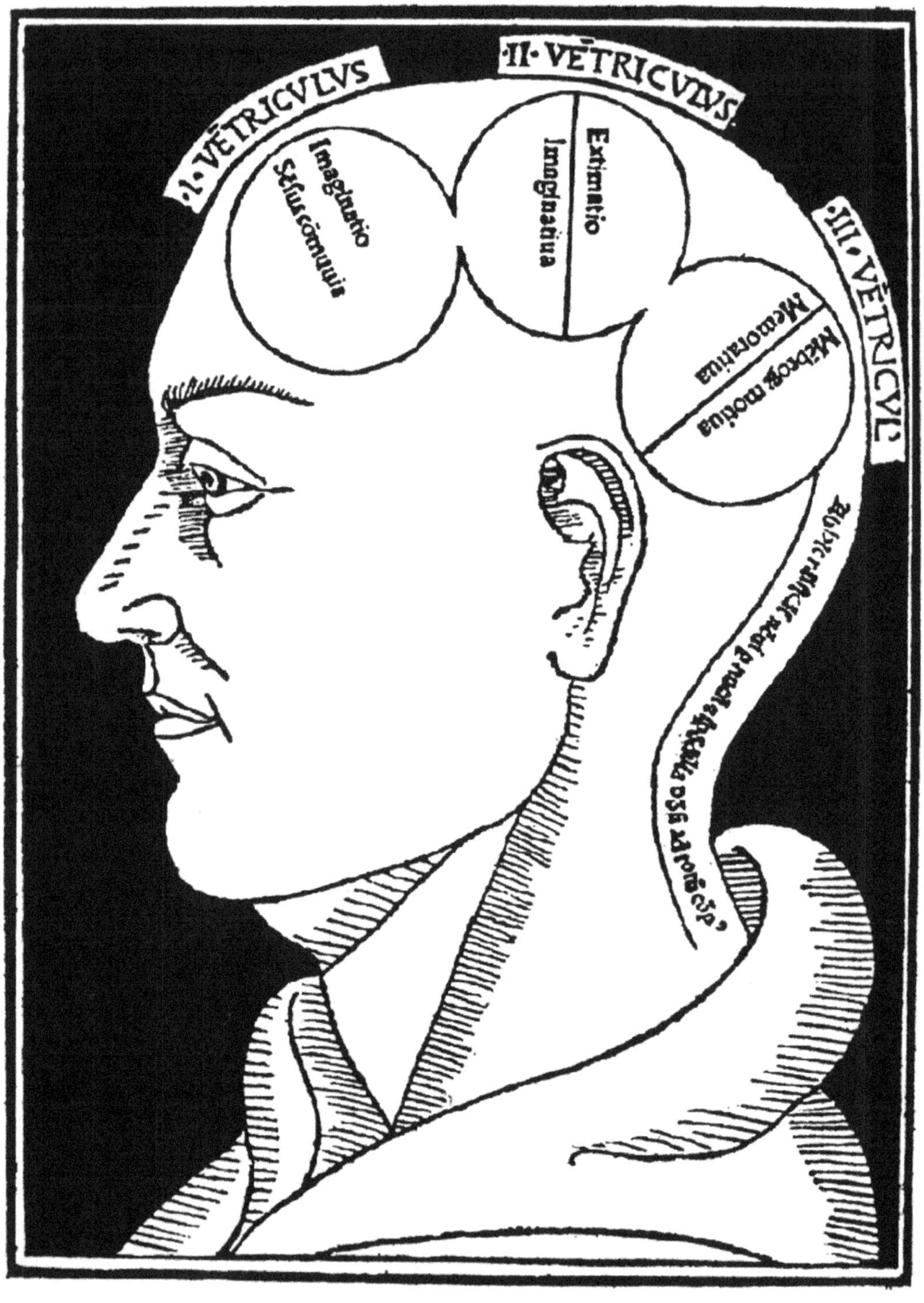

Figure 2.

From Albertus Magnus,

Philosophia Naturalis

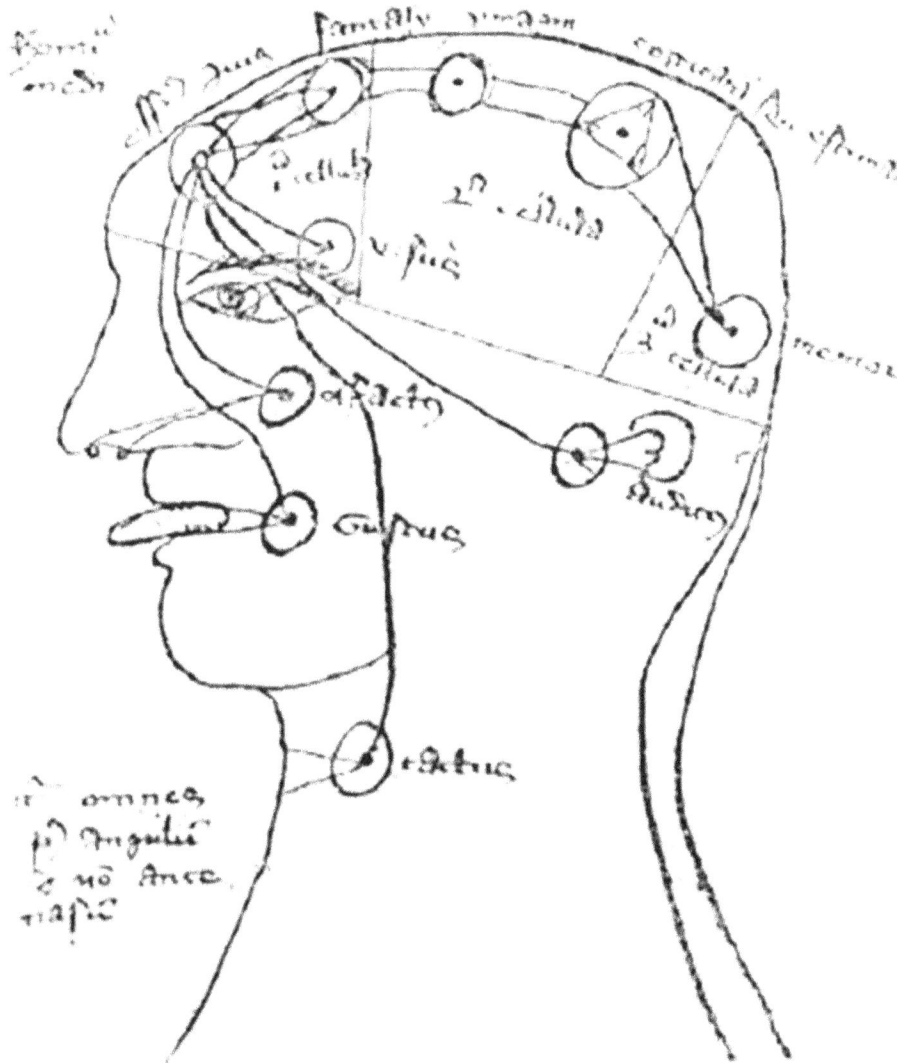

Figure 3.

From Avicenna, De generatione embryonis. Around the cranium is inscribed,
"sensus conmunis, fantasia, ymaginativa, cogitativa seu estimativa, memorativa

8. *The Interior Senses.* There are five groups of interior faculties: the composite, the imagination, the apprehensive or instinct, the retentive or memory, and the ratiocinative. The first two are taken together by the physician [Galen], but not by the philosopher [Aristotle].

9. *The Composite sense. Common sense: Hiss-i-mushtarik)* is that which receives all forms and images perceived by the external senses, and combines them (into one common mental picture).

10. *Imagination.* (Phantasy). This preserves the percepts of the composite sense after they have been so conjoined, and holds them after the sense-impressions have subsided. The common sense is the recipient and the imaginatlon is the preserver. The proof of this belongs to the philosopher.

11. The chief seat of the activities of these two faculties ls the anterior part of the braln.

12. *The Cogitatlve Faculty.* The faculty which medicine calls cogitative is taken in two senses in philosophy. It is regarded sometimes as "Imaginative faculty" [*mutakhayyal,* animal] and sometimes as "cogitative faculty." [*mutafakkira:* human]. in the view of the philosopher, the former is where the appre- hensive faculty comes into play, and the latter is where reason controls or decides that a given action is advantageous. There is also the difference that the imagination deals with sense-form percepts, whereas the cogitation uses the percepts which have been stored in the imagination and then proceeds to combine and analyse them, and construct quite different Images: e.g., a flying man, an emerald mountain. The imagination does not present to you anything but what it already received through the sense organs.

13. The seat of this faculty is in the midportion of the brain.

14. *The Apprehensive Faculty.* This faculty is the instrument of the power called instinct in animals ("Animal prudence"). By it, for instance, an animal knows that a wolf is an enemy, and the kid distinguishes its dam as a friend from whom he need not flee. Such a decision is not formed by the reasoning powers, but is another mode of apprehension. Friendship and enmity are not perceived by the senses, nor do the senses comprehend them; and they are not perceived by the reason either. Man employs the same faculty on very many occasions exactly as does an irrational animal.

15. The Retentive Faculty. Memory (*Hafiza Dhakira*). The power of memory is as it were a treasury or repository for those supra-sensuous ideas discovered by the apprehensive faculty, just as the imagination is the treasury or repository for the sense-impressions of forms and sensible images (formed by the common sense). The seat of this faculty is in the postertor region of the brain.[30]

Magnus' and Avicenna's versions of the ventricular theory of brain function were among many such theories in the Middle Ages.

The most complete comparison of a representative sampling of the theories was made by Walter Sudhoff in 1913 (see Figure 4).[31] Inspection of the chart reveals more similarities than differences since all of them are various versions of Nemesius' original theory.

When Avicenna's and Magnus' versions of the ventricular theory became available to the Christian West, various Encyclopedists tried to reconcile their differences in composite illustrations. One such example is seen in Figure 5, from the 1496 edition of the *Epitomata* of Gerard de Harderwyck.[32] The upper two heads show the usual divisions and labeling of brain functions followed by adherents to the ventricular theory, but the one on the left is said to represent the writings of Galen and Avicenna, and the one on the right is said to accord with the theories of St. Thomas Aquinas and Albertus Magnus.

The lower figure in the illustration is of particular interest because it depicts not only the various cranial divisions, but also the various senses impinging upon the first cell to create the *"sensus commmunis."* The connections between the ear, the first cell and the heart illustrate the Aristotelian doctrine that the heart, not the brain, is the chief organ of the body and seat of the soul.

Vesalius and the Rediscovery of Galen

In the middle of the 16th century, the ventricular localization of psychological function was still being taught to physicians, for Vesalius in *De humani corporls fabrlca* mentions how he had been made to learn it:

> I well remember that when in the University of Louvain in the *Pedagogium Castrense*—easily the leading and most distinguished college—I gave my efforts to philosophy. In those commentaries on Aristotle's *De anlma*, then read to us by our teacher, a theologian by profession and therefore, like the other instructors at that Academy, ready to mingle his own pious views with those of the philosophers—the brain was said to have been equipped with three ventricles. The first was in front, the second in the middle, the third behind, with names according to their position and other names derived from their functions.
>
> The first or frontal, said to lie towards the forehead, was the ventricle of 'Common Sense' (sensus communis) since, as they believed, from it the nerves of the five senses pass to their instruments. It was by these nerves that smell, colour, taste, sound, and touch were said to be led to that ventricle. Accordingly, the main use of this first ventricle was to receive the objects of the five senses of the kind that we generally call "Common Sense."

C. Arthur Ellis, Jr.

	ginaria		
Joannes Damaskenos	φαντασιχόν	διανοητιχόν	μνημονευτιχόν
Costa ben Luca	sensus, phantasia	intellectus cogitatio providentia cognitio	memoria motus
Razes	imaginatio	cogitatio	memoria
Haly Abbas	phantasia	cogitatio	memoria
Die lauteren Brüder	Vorstellungskraft (phantasia)	Denkkraft (cogitatio)	Gedächtnis (memoria)
Avicenna	sensus communis phantasia	cogitativa imaginativa existimatio	conservativa memorialis
Constantinus Africanus	sensus phantasia	intellectus ratio	motus memoria
Copho	phantasia	ratio	memoria
Adelard v. Bath	phantasia	ratio	memoria
Avenzoar	imaginativa	cogitativa	memoria
Averrues	sensus communis imaginatio	cogitativa extimativa	reminiscibilis conservativa
Algazel	sensus communis imaginativa	imaginativa cogitativa	aestimativa memoria
Wilhelm von Conches	cellula phantastica	cellula logistica sive rationalis	cellula memorialis
Richardus Salernitanus	cellula phantastica, imaginatio	cellula logistica ratio	cellula memorialis memoria
Albert der Grosse[1)	sensus communis imaginatio phantasia et estimativa	existamativa (imaginativa) cogitativa formativa	memorativa virtus motiva
Thomas von Aquino	sensus communis phantasia sive imaginatio	existimativa cogitativa	memorativa
Ricardus Anglicus	operationes sensibiles	ymaginationes cogitationes	
Wilhelm von Saliceto	sensus communis phantasia imaginatio	cogitatio existimatio	memoria
Lanfranc	sensus communis ymaginativa phantasia	aestimativa	conservat sententias pronuntiatas (memoria)
Heinrich von Mondeville	sensus communis ymaginativa	aestimativa	secreta thesaurizat (memoria)

Figure 4.

Survey of various ventricular theories of brain function.

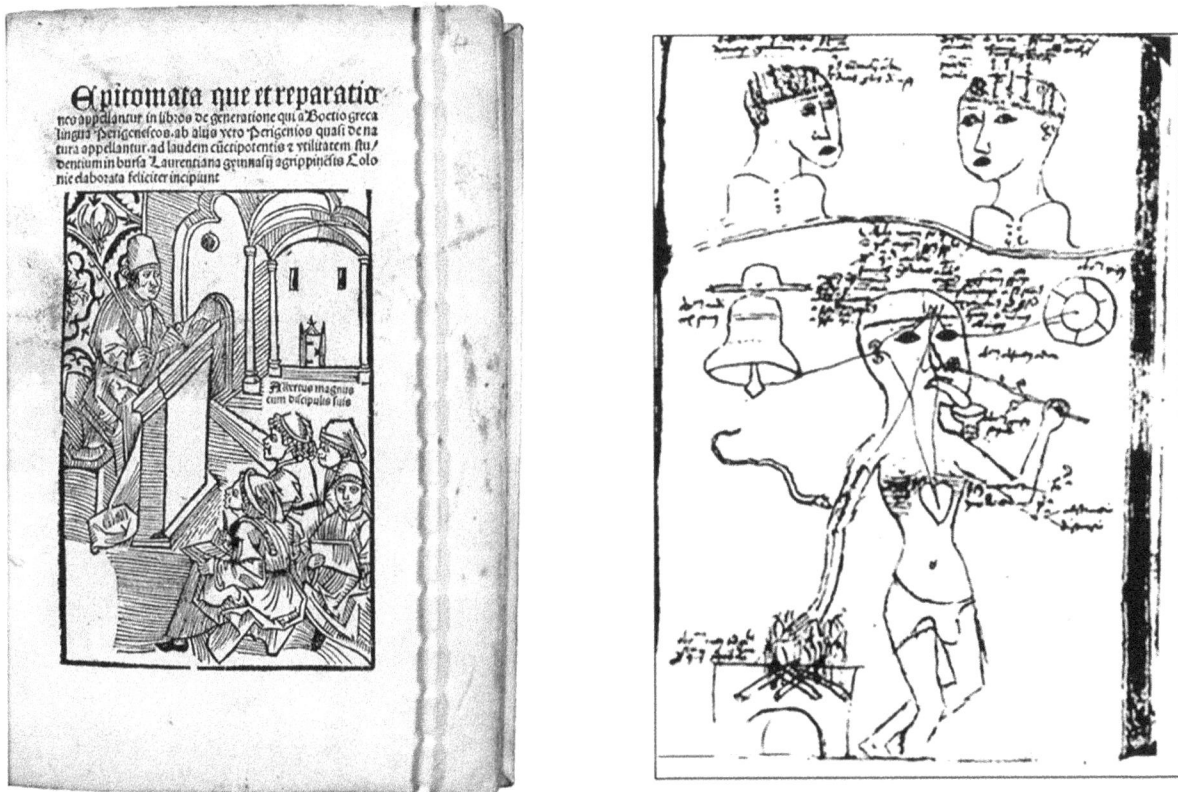

Figure 5.

Cover and an illustration from 1496 edition of Gerard Harderwyck's

Epitomata preserved at the University of Glasgow.

This ventricle was linked to the second ventricle by a certain passage through which these objects pass. Thus the second ventricle could imagine, meditate, and consider the objects in question; for to this ventricle Thought and Reason were ascribed.

The third ventricle was dedicated to Memory. The second ventricle would, according to its nature, pass to it all those things which it wished to be entrusted thereto, namely those objects upon which it had thoroughly meditated. And moreover the third ventricle, accordingly as it was more moist or dry, would either more quickly or more slowly grave those things upon itself, as upon wax or [more thoroughly] upon stone. Further, those Commentaries teach that, according to the ease or difficulty of the engraving, this ventricle would preserve that which it receives for a shorter or for a longer time. Yet this ventricle neither retains nor incises those things for itself nor by its own right, but for the sake of the second ventricle. And so, forsooth, whensoever the second ventricle sets out to meditate on something confided to the bosom of Memory, [the third ventricle] speedily returns (*exporrigat*) that thing into the second ventricle and there distributes it as into a workshop of Reason, as something which should there abide.

That we should follow up more in detail the items which we were thus taught, we were shown a figure from some *Philosophic Pearl* which presented to the eyes the ventricles so discussed. This figure we pupils portrayed, each according to his skills as draughtsman, adding it to our notes. It was suggested to us that this figure comprehended not merely the three ventricles but all relevant parts of the head, and especially of the brain.[33]

The figure which Vesalius traced in his student notes is given in Figure 6, from the Margarita Phllosophlca (Pearl of Wisdom), an encyclopedia published by Gregor Reisch in 1503.[34] As Vesalius' career progressed from the tracing of traditional ventricular figures as a student to independent investigation of the structure of the brain (Figure 7), he wrote the following about the speculative physiology he was taught:

Such are the inventions of those who never look into our Maker's ingenuity in the building of the human body!

....

But what impiety can such a description of the uses of the ventricles (as it concerns the powers of the Reigning Soul) produce in ignorant minds not yet confirmed in our Most Holy Religion![35]

On the basis of his own anatomical work, and the observation that beasts as well as men share the commonality of ventricles in the brain, Vesalius continues by rejecting the ventricular localization of the "faculties" of the rational soul:

> For such [ignorant ones] will examine carefully (even though I myself were silent) the brains of quadrupeds. These closely resemble those of men in all their parts. Should we on that account ascribe to these [beasts] every power of reason, and even a rational soul, on the basis of such doctrines of the theologlans?[36]

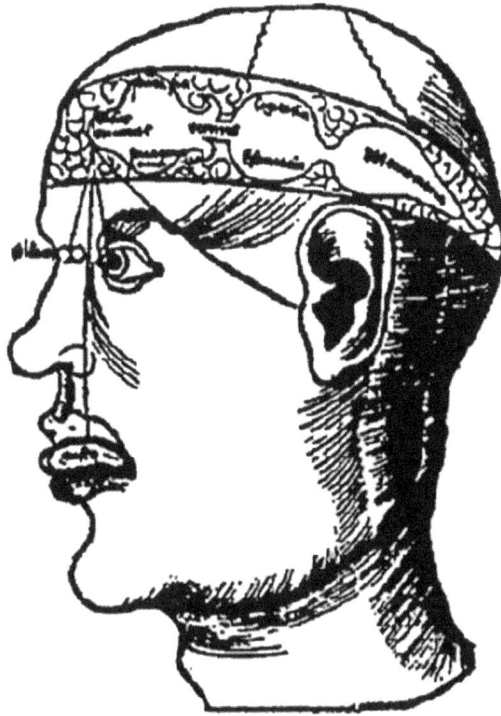

Figure 6.

Diagram of the brain and its relations to the senses and intellectual faculties from Reisch, *Margarita Philosophica* (Strasburg, 1504). On the brain are written the following:

	Fantasia		Cogitative	
Sensus			Vermis	Memorativa
Communis				
	Imaginativa			Estimativa

These occupy positions on the three traditional ventricles. To the *sensus communis* converge nerves from the ear, eye, nose (olfactus) and mouth (gustus).

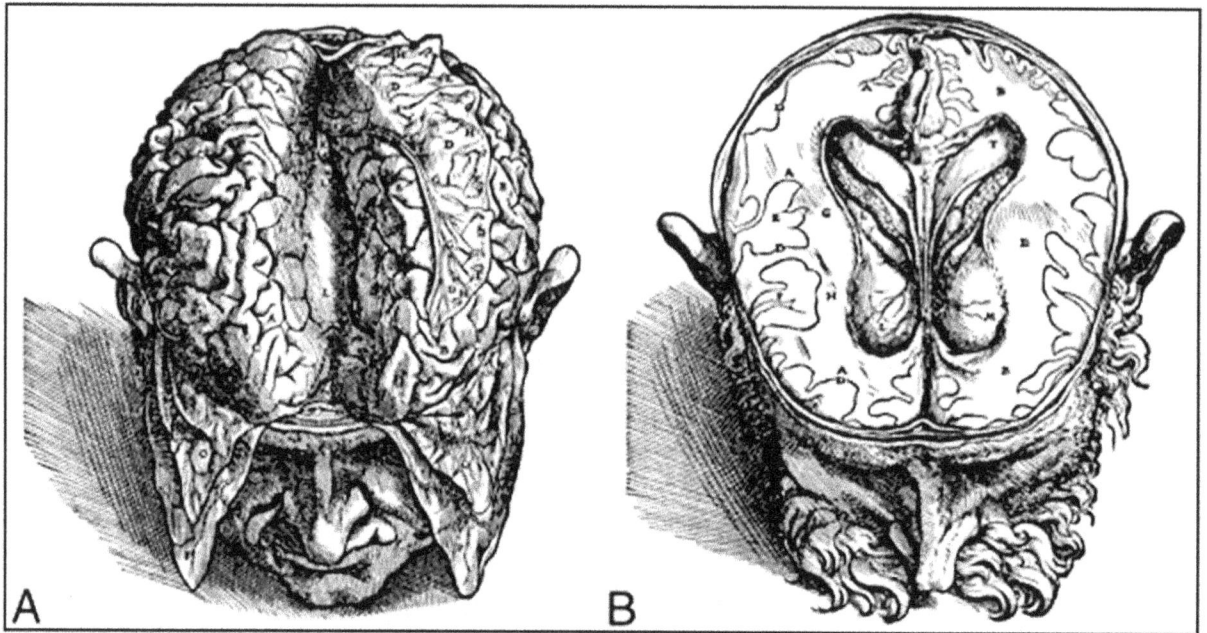

Figure 7.

Vesalius, De humani carporis fabrlca.

Figures are part of a series in which Vesalius illustrates the progressive approach to revealing the ventricles by cutting and peeling back flaps made in the brain.

As to the physiological role of the ventricles of the brain, Vesalius writes:

> What I put down here on the use of the brain I have discussed cursorily at the beginning of this Book. There I ventured to ascribe no more to the ventricles than that they are cavities and spaces in which the inhaled air, added to the vital spirit from the heart, is, by power of the peculiar substance of the brain, transformed into animal splrit.[37]

Vesalius' description of the role of the ventricles departs from Nemesius' view and returns to the account of brain function given by Galen, especially in his statement that "vital spirit, transmitted to them [the ventricles] by the heart, are altered by the power of the peculiar substance of the brain into animal spirit."

Galen's faculties are again brought into play, and the body becomes once again physiological, as opposed to spiritual, in its functioning.

In a discussion of Vesalius' indebtedness to Galen, the great historian of medicine, Charles Singer, writes:

In estimating the anatomical standpoint of Vesalius, too much has sometimes been made of his "anti-Galenism." In this connexion it must be remembered that in the very years in which he was most busily occupied on the *Fabrica* the leisure of Vesalius was largely devoted to editing Galenic works. His *Talulae sex* and his edition of Galen in Latin are still of value for the study of that author. One of the contributors to it was Vesalius, who edited the works, *On the dissection of the nerves, On the dissection of the veins and arteries*, and the great treatise *On anatomical procedure.*

Moreover, the numberless references to Galen in the *Fabrlca* exhibit the respect of the Reformer of Anatomy for the opinion of the Prince of Physicians. Of a truth it was hardly open to Vesalius to do other than build on Galen. The Galenic works, now accessible in good recent versions to which Vesalius himself had thus contributed, presented by far the best current anatomical accounts. The tone of much of the criticism of Galen is not, it is true, that which a modern writer would adopt. This we must put down to the custom of the tlme.[38]

In regard to Vesalius' dependence upon Galen's description of the brain, Singer notes:

Emphasis is laid by Vesalius on the pituitary gland and its fossa. Especially he deals with the supposed relation to the rete mirabile, the existence of which he does not wholly reject. His figure of this structure, he says, is made to fit the description of Galen![40]

Anatomy and Physiology in the Renaissance

A striking characteristic of the Renaissance is that it was marked by the swift rise of anatomy and the comparatively slow development of physiology, a fact that is not at all surprising since anatomy depends primarily upon empirical observation while physiology requires the additional element of a philosophical or theoretical framework within which the anatomical findings are interpreted.

Thus, discrepancies between what was described by earlier anatomists and what was found to be true upon direct observation could only be explained by hypothesizing new physiological models. A case in point is the discovery of the circulation of the blood: Vesalius' note of the lack of inter-ventricular pores, coupled with Fabrlcius' description of the valves in the veins, were used by Harvey in his model of the circulatory system.

But in regard to the structure and function of the brain, developments in anatomy were much more rapid than theories of brain function to accommodate the new observations. The fact that Vesalius adhered to Galen's account of brain function as opposed to the ventricular doctrine has already been discussed, and is paralleled by the work of Leonardo Da Vinci. Da Vinci, from his work with cast bronzes, turned to the anatomical study of the human brain, injecting the ventricles with hot wax and teasing away the surrounding tissue.[41] The result, shown in Figure 9, contrasts markedly with the earlier drawings of he brain he had made prior to conducting his own dissections (Figure 8).

The advance in anatomical accuracy made possible by this new technique was not paralleled by a new theory of brain function, however, and Leonardo's work was lost to the world until the twentieth century.[42]

In conclusion, while advances were made by Da Vinci in the anatomical accuracy of portraying the human brain during the Renaissance, the only progress made in understanding the physiology of the brain was in returning to the physical, Galenic interpretation of brain function as opposed to the prevailing philological view founded upon the writings of Nemesius. Furthermore, the Galenic interpretation of brain function employed vitalistic explanations, which depended upon various undefined "faculties" and "sympathies," which were not subject to experimentation.

Until investigation of the human body could be conducted within the framework of a more material, non-psychistic philosophy, advances in medical knowledge were at a standstill.

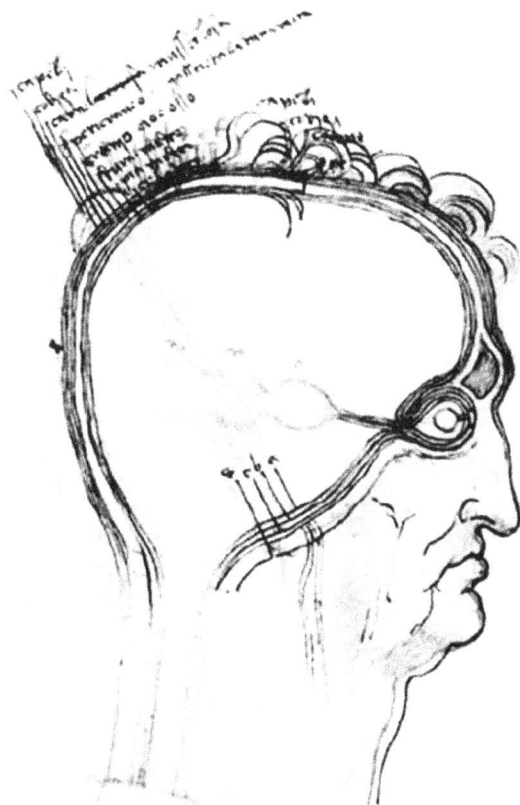

Figure 8.
Da Vinci's illustration of the Ventricular Doctrine based upon various philosophical writings.

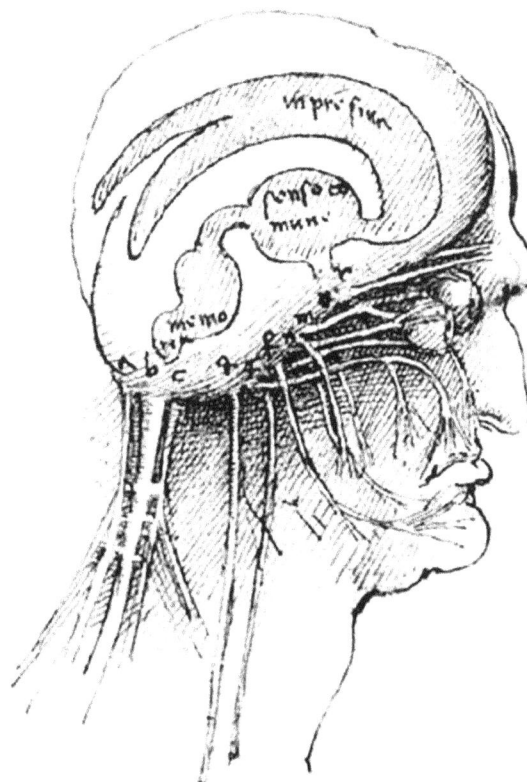

Figure 9.
Da Vinci's illustration of his anatomical findings following injection of wax and teasing away surrounding tissue.

Notes to Chapter 1

[1] George Sarton, The Appreciation of Ancient and Medieval Science During the Renaissance (Philadelphia: University of Pennsylvania Press, 1955), p. 50.

[2] Galen, On the Usefulness of the Parts of the Body, trans. from the Greek with an Introduction and Commentary by Margaret Tallmadge May, 2 vols. (New York: Cornell University Press, 1968). May's extensive Introduction is excellent, especially the section which begins on page 44 of Volume I, entitled "Galen's System of Physiology."

[3] May, p. 45.

[4] May, p. 45.

[5] Galen, On the Natural Faculties, trans. Arthur John Brock, in Great Books of the Western World, Vol. 10, ed. Robert Maynard Hutchins (Chicago: Encyclopedia Britannica, 1952), p. 167.

[6] Galen shared the belief, common among philosophers from earliest recorded history until well within the Renaissance, that animate motion was due to a soul. For a thorough discussion of this concept, see T. S. Hall's Ideas of Life and Matter.

[7] Galen's discussion of the pneumatic philosophy may be found in his On the Usefulness of the Parts of the Body, beginning on page 204 of the May edition. Charles J. Singer, in The Evolution of Anatomy (New York: Alfred A. Knopf, 1925), also gives an excellent discussion of the concept on pp. 58-62.

[8] A discussion of the divisions of the soul and their associated faculties is found in May's translation of Galen's On the Usefulness of the Parts of the Body, pp. 49-50. Also, "faculty" is contained in the index of the work, facilitating access to Galen's many references to the word. Of course, the major work by Galen discussing his idea of faculties is his On the Natural Faculties.

[9] This philosophy is evident in all sections of On the Usefulness of the Parts of the Body and On the Natural Faculties.

[10] *On the Natural Faculties*, p. 169.

[11] See May, pp. 51-53 for a discussion of Galen's notion of innate heat.

[12] The illustration and general description of Galen's physiology which follows are adapted from Singer, *The Evolution of Anatomy*, pp. 58-62.

[13] Galen, *On the Usefulness of the Parts of the Body*, pp. 389-390.

[14] Galen, p. 391.

[15] Galen, *On Anatomical Procedures*, trans. W. L. Duckworth as *Galen on Anatomical Procedures, The Later Books*, ed. M. C. Lyons and B. Towers (Cambridge: Cambridge University Press, 1962), pp. 18-19.

[16] Galen, *The Sites of Diseases*, quoted by Edwin Clarke and C. D. O'Malley, *The Human Brain and Spinal Cord: A Historical Study Illustrated by Writings from Antiquity to the Twentieth Century* (Berkeley: University of California Press, 1968), pp. 461-462. The passage is translated from Charles V. Daremberg, *Oeuvres anatomiques, physiologiques et médicales de Galien, traduites sur les textes imprimés et manuscrits, accompagnées de sommaires, de notes, de planches et d'une table des matières, precédées d'une introduction ou étude biographique, littéraire et scientifique sur Galien* (Paris: J. B. Bailliere, 1854-1856), II, pp. 561-562.

[17] Galen, *The Differentiation of Symptoms*, quoted by Clarke and O'Malley, p. 462, trans. from C. G. Kuhn, *Claudii Galeni opera omnia* (Leipzig: Cnobloch, 1821-1833), Vol. VII, pp. 55-56.

[18] Galen, *The Differentiation of Symptoms*, Kuhn edition, pp. 60-62.

[19] William Telfer, *Cyril of Jerusalem and Nemesius of Emesa*, The Library of Christian Classics, Vol. IV (Philadelphia: The Westminster Press, 1940), pp. 203-211, gives an account of what is known of Nemesius' life. The text also contains a translation of Nemesius' only work, *Of the Nature of Man*, along with an extensive commentary. All subsequent references to Nemesius' work will be to this edition.

[20] Telfer, p. 218.

[21] Nemesius, p. 226.

[22] Nemesius, p. 319.

[23] Nemesius, p. 321.

[24] Nemesius, p. 341.

[25] Telfer, pp. 216-223.

[26] See Edwin Clarke and Kenneth Dewhurst, An Illustrated History of Brain Function (Berkeley: University of California Press, 1972), pp. 10-50.

[27] Clarke and Dewhurst, p. 23.

[28] Clarke and Dewhurst, p. 30.

[29] The ventricular doctrine is elaborated by Avicenna in On the Soul, trans. by F. Rahman in Avicenna's Psychology: An English Translation of Kitab Al-Najat, Book II, Chapter VI with Historico-Philosophical Notes and Textual Improvements on the Cairo Edition (London: Oxford University Press, 1952).

[30] Avicenna, Canon of Medicine, trans. O. C. Gruner in A Treatise on the Canon of Medicine of Avicenna Incorporating a Translation of the First Book (London: n.p., 1930), excerpts from pp. 134-138.

[31] Walter Sudhoff, "Die Lehre von den Hirnventrikeln in textlicher und graphischer Tradition des Altertums und Mittelalters," Archiv für Geschichte der Medizin, 7, No. 3 (1913), 11-205. The table is reproduced from pp. 179-180 of the article.

[32] This figure appears on a blank leaf preceding the printed work "De sensu" in the encyclopedic work entitled Epitomate, by Gerard de Harderwyk (d. 1503), first printed in 1496. A print and translation of the writing on the plate was supplied courtesy of the Trustees of the Wellcome Historical Medical Library, London.

[33] Andreas Vesalius, De humani corporis fabrica, portions trans. by Charles Singer as Vesalius on the Human Brain (London: Oxford Univesity Press, 1952), pp. 5-6.

[34] Gregor Reisch, Margarita Philosophica (Freiburg im Breisgau: J. Schott, 1503), fig. 18; rpt. with discussion in Clarke and Dewhurst, An Illustrated History of Brain Function, figure 48, p. 34.

35 Vesalius, Singer edition, p. 6; Figure 7 reproduced from p. 99.

36 Vesalius, p. 6.

37 Vesalius, p. 39.

38 Charles Singer, The Evolution of Anatomy, p. 119. For a later article by Singer on the subject of Vesalius' dependence on Galen, see "Some Galenic and Animal Sources of Vesalius," Journal of the History of Medicine and Allied Sciences, 1, No. 1 (1946), pp. 6-24.

39 Singer, The Evolution of Anatomy, p. 132.

40 Figures 8 and 9, along with a thorough discussion of daVinci's work on the human body appears in C. D. O'Malley and J. B. Saunders, Leonardo da Vinci on the Human Body (New York: Henry Schuman, 1952). See also, Charles Singer, "Notes on Renaissance Artists and Practical Anatomy," Journal of the History of Medicine and Allied Sciences, 5 (1950), pp. 156-162; and W. H. Magoun, "Development of Ideas Relating to Mind with the Brain," in The Historical Development of Physiological Thought (New York: Hafner, 1959), pp. 81-105.

CHAPTER 2:

THE REJECTION OF VITALISM IN THE 17TH CENTURY

In one of his dialogues written in the 17th century, Guglielmini recorded the following edifying tableau of contemporary medical controversies:

> Sixty years ago, when I was young…it was only a question of innate heat, of radical humidity, of first qualities and other similar things; for anatomy, one followed Riolan or Nexling, who were at the time new authors; for botany, J. Bauhin; for practical work, Sennert and Riviere…the theory of the circulation of the blood was mere rumour. I was barely up to date with all of this…when people began to speak of the chemical system of Van Helmont, then of that of Sylvius and of Willis…even the physiologists, imagining that they should share a common cause with physlcians, repudiating the ideas of Aristotle, introduced into medicine the systems of Descartes and of Gassendi, systems which had been twisted to the point that no one which physiological foundation each physician based his theories and instituted his treatments. Was not this diversity of doctrines enough to confound everything without counting the mathematicians who ended up by embroiling everything even more? If you understand well what I have said, Cleobule my friend, you will remain persuaded that all of this did not come from the desire to progress and perfect the arts, but from a disorganized mania of producing novelties, and from vainglory.[1]

Regardless of Guglielmini's opinion regarding motives, the 17th century marked a turning point from the earlier vitalistic, mystical accounts of life prevalent throughout the Middle Ages to the practically-oriented, experientially-based explanations beginning about the time of Vesalius. Furthermore, while a number of medical thinkers of the late 16th and early 17th centuries openly challenged vitalistic theories, the majority, although accepting such views, tended to evoke them less and less—Aristotelian and Galenic ideas were beginning to suffer erosion.2

Vitalistic Explanations of Life Phenomena

T. S. Hall notes in his translation of Descartes' *Treatise of Man* that there are five physiological "isms" prevalent among vitalist explanations of life phenomena that persisted into the time of Vesalius, which 17th century medical thought would challenge:

1. Humoralism: the "Hippocratic" assumption that the body comprises four humors, whose different blends or temperaments are responsible for the functions of the different organs.
2. Dualism of body and spirit: the Stoic (and alchemical) idea that all things, including living things, consist of both body (soma) and spirit (pneuma); or often, in alchemical thought, "quintessence."
3. Pneumatism: the neo-Galenic assumption of three spirits or pneumata—animal, vital, and natural.
4. Interpretation in terms of "faculties": the Galenic use of undefined "faculties" to explain unknown physiological functions in terms of their qualities.
5. Animism, or psychism: the attribution of all the patent manifestations of life to a latent causal entity, the psyche or life-soul.[3]

Of the foregoing, animism (the attribution of the outward manifestations of life functions to a soul) is perhaps the most ancient; and the belief that the soul is responsible for movement in living things goes back as far as recorded history.[4]

Aristotle had made motion the distinctive property of living things, and that idea continued unchallenged for centuries. No less a scientist than Kepler believed the stars to be animated because of their apparent movement, and Gilbert was convinced that magnets had souls because of their ability to move and be moved. Hearing of the work of Copernicus, maintaining the movement of the earth, Thomas Campanella, writing behind prison walls, exclaimed, "Mundum esse animal, totum sentiens!"[5] In a world so alive and sentient, motion was seen as a manifestation of a "world soul", present in all life forms, from the least to the greatest, forming an unbroken "Great Chain of Being."[6]

Vitalistic philosophy was especially to be found in explanations of life functions by physicians and physiologists well into the 17th century, with William Harvey being one of the better known vitalists. A recently discovered manuscript by Harvey, described below by Julian Jaynes, is particularly revealing of Harvey's vitalist explanations of life functions:

> The physiology is essentially Galenic in its resort to animal spirits but breaks off into exasperated splurges of metaphor. The brain in particular is compared to a choirmaster,

who performs behavior with an exquisite sense of rhythm and harmony. When the brain was removed—and here he cut off the head of a chicken and watched its behavior to prove it—behavior is disorderly, for muscles are like separate living creatures which have to be directed in harmony by the choirmaster of the brain. And from this metaphor, too, comes his emphasis on rhythm in muscular coordination, how each muscular system has a sub-rhythm of tension and relaxation, just as the beat of the heart has its systole and diastole.[7]

Jaynes concludes:

> The notebook ends with a list of metaphors which might generate some kind of truth. The choirmaster model is reiterated, or the heart is compared to a general or king, the brain to a judge or sergeant-major, the nerves to leaders or magistrates, and the muscles to soldiers—all, be it noted, enclosed within the animal without relating to its environment. A new metaphor through which to "see" behavior was indeed needed before any further progress could be made.[8]

But it is not necessary to search notebooks to find Harvey's vitalist descriptions of bodily functions, since his own account, in *De Hotu Cordis,* of the circulation of the blood, is very revealing:

> I began to think whether there might not be a motion as it were in a circle. Now this I afterwards found to be true…which motion we may be allowed to call circular, in the same way as Aristotle says that the air and the rain emulate the circular motion of the superior bodies; for the moist earth, warmed by the sun, evaporates; the vapours drawn upwards are condensed, and descending in the form of rain moisten the earth again; and by this arrangement are generations of living things produced; and in like manner too are tempests and meteors engendered by the circular motion, and by the approach and recession of the sun. And so in all likelihood does it come to pass in the body through the motion of the blood; the various parts are nourished, cherished, quickened by the warmer more perfect vaporous spiritous and as I may say alimentive blood; which, on the contrary, in contact with these parts, becomes cooled, coagulated and so to speak effects; whence it returns to its sovereign, the heart, as if to its source, or to the inmost home of the body, there to recover its state of excellence or perfection. Here it resumes its due fluidity and receives an infusion of natural heat—powerful, fervid, a kind of treasury of life, and is impregnated with spirits, and it might be said, with the balsam,

and thence it is again dispersed; and all this depends on the motion and action of the heart. The heart, consequently, is the beginning of life; the sun of the microcosm, even as the sun in its turn might well be described as the heart of the world; for it is the heart which…is indeed the foundation of life, the source of all action.[9]

The analogies here are political (the heart as the monarch) and domestic (the heart as the restoring fireside). The heart is also the treasury, providing the blood with a refurbished currency. Harvey sees the circulation of the blood as a recurring cycle of vapour and moisture, an "arrangement by which generations of living things are produced." Both in its metaphors and in its assignment of the controlling functions of life to the heart, the description is interpreted within the Aristotelian world picture.

Descartes' Traité de l'homme: The Mechanistic Alternative to Vitalist Explanations of Life Phenomena

Since the pioneering studies of Boas and Dijksterhuis, the shift away from "vitalist" Interpretations of life phenomena—involving faculties, substantial forms, and *animae*—to a "mechanical interpretation—involving contact forces, particulate motions, and mechanical and hydraulic models—has been viewed primarily as the result of a gradual and evolutionary "mechanization of the world picture."[8]

The Greeks, for example, compared the movement of automata to the movement of animals, and as early as the 14th century, when clocks worked by wheels were still new, it was suggested that the stars were actually a piece of clockwork. In the Middle Ages, Albertus Magnus (ca. 1200-80) had in his laboratory at Cologne a robot that could move and give a greeting, saying *salve* (hail).

Sloan, differing with this gradualist Interpretation, contrasts the work of Harvey and Descartes to demonstrate that the genesis of the Cartesian variety of physiological mechanism at least cannot be considered a product of the incursion of a pre-existent tradition of mechanics into biology."[11] In support of this, Sloan quotes a 17th century anatomist who recognized Descartes' radical mechanical view of human physiology:

Descartes…was the first who dared to explain all the functions of man, and especially of the brain, in a mechanical manner. Other authors describe man; Descartes puts before us merely a machine, but by means of this he very clearly exposed the ignorance of others who have treated of man, and opened up for us a way by which to investigate the use of the other parts of the body as no one has done before.[12]

Since this early recognition of the value of the mechanistic hypothesis to the study of the human body, numerous scholars have furnished convincing evidence to support the claim, voiced by Jaynes, that "one of the great turning points in science was when man-made machines became the hypotheses or models of natural phenomena."[13]

Certainly Descartes' description of life phenomena, especially in his *Traité de l'homrne,* is radically mechanistic, as recognized by Dijksterhuis:

> In Descartes, this principal meaning of mechanistic—with the aid of mechanics—already involved to some extent the later connotation of the word, namely capable of being imitated in a mechanical model. As a matter of fact, he states explicitly that between natural bodies and artefacts produced by skillful artisans he recognizes no other difference than one of size: that which takes place invisibly in the former, in the latter happens on so big a scale that we can observe it. For the rest, there is not a single difference between a running clockwork and a growing tree. That is also why those who are versed in the construction of automata are best fitted to guess the true process of natural phenomena, the mechanisms hidden in them.[14]

The radical mechanism to which Dljksterhuis refers ls quite evident in the closing section of the *Traite de l'homme*:

> I desire you to consider, further, that all the functions that I have attributed to this machine, such as the digestion of food; the beating of the heart and arteries; the nourishment and growth of the members; respiration; waking and sleeping; the reception by the external sense organs of light, sounds, smells, tastes, heat, and all other such qualities; the imprinting of the ideas of these qualities in the organ of common sense and imagination; the retention or imprint of these Ideas in the memory; the internal movements of the appetites and passions; and finally, the external movements of all the members that so properly follow both the actions of objects presented to the senses and the passions and impressions which are entailed in the memory—I desire you to consider, I say, that these functions imitate those of a real man as perfectly as possible and that they follow naturally in this machine entirely from the disposition of the organs—no more nor less than do the movements of its counterweights and wheels. Wherefore it is not necessary, on their account, to conceive of any vegetative or sensitive soul or any other principle of movement and life than its blood and its spirits, agitated by the heat of the fire which burns continually in its heart and which is of no other nature than all those fires that occur in animate bodles.[15]

In this description of physiological functions within the human body, Descartes follows not the traditional or neoclassical account of such writers as Fernet or Riolan, but a relentless application of the laws of mechanics to life phenomena. As Brown notes, "Descartes wields Ockham's razor to strip away excess souls, faculties, forces, and innate heats from the corpuscular or chemical core of explanation."[16]

This mechanistic, reductionistic view of all phenomena, including life itself, was the outgrowth of Descartes' philosophy, and his primary contribution to the history of science. Often overlooked by scholars is the fact that Descartes' science grew hand in hand with his philosophy, as recognized by Sloan, who states, "Descartes' philosophical and scientific thought forms a coherent unity in which we can make no distinctions between a 'philosophical' and 'scientific' Descartes;" and Brown, who states that "Descartes' physiology grew and developed as an integral part of his philosophy."[17]

The Cartesian metaphysic was intended to establish an absolute, unshakable foundation for scientific work—a recurrent theme encountered in all of Descartes' basic "philosophical" works: the *Rules* (1628), the *Discourse* (1639), and the *Principles* (1644). Descartes' belief that uncertainty in first principles and inadequate philosophical grounding of the sciences was the cause of their slow and confused development is apparent in the following passage from the *Rules*:

> Science in its entirety is true and evident cognition. He ls no more learned who has doubts on many matters than the man who has never thought of them; nay he appears to be less learned if he has formed wrong opinions on any particulars. Hence it were better not to study at all than to occupy one's self with objects of such difficulty, that owing to our inability to distinguish true from false, we are forced to regard the doubtful as certain; for in those matters any hope of augmenting our knowledge is exceeded by the risk of diminishing it. Thus in accordance with the above maxim we reject all such merely probable knowledge and make it a rule to trust only what is completely known and incapable of being doubted.[18]

Descartes' physiology, too, grew alongside his philosophical development. In the twelfth *regula*, written early in his career, Descartes maintained that all animal and subrational human movements are controlled solely by unconscious mechanisms. Today, we know that these subconscious functions are performed by the autonomic nervous system.

Elsewhere in the *Regulae*, Descartes maintains that all phenomena of the animate and inanimate world, with the single exception of those necessitating the intervention of the human will and consciousness, are to be explained in terms of mathematics, matter, configuration, and motion.

Following the initial statement of animal automatism in the *Regulae*, Descartes set out to study animals as thoroughly as possible, as is seen from a little-known account of his experimental activities in 1629, taken from Baillet's biography:

In this conviction, he set about the execution of his design by studying anatomy, to which he devoted the whole of the winter that he spent in Amsterdam. To Father Mersenne he testified that his eagerness for knowledge of this subject had made him visit, almost daily, a butcher, to witness the slaughter; and that he had caused to be brought thence to his dwelling whichever of the animal's organs he desired to dissect at greater leisure. He often did the same thing in other places where he stayed after that, finding nothing personally shameful, or unworthy of his position, in a practice that was innocent in itself and that could produce quite useful results. Thus he made fun of certain maleficent and envious persons who, intending to enjoy themselves at the expense of his reputation, had tried to make him out a criminal and had accused him of "going through the villages to see pigs killed," although this was absolutely false so far as the villages were concerned.

He read little at this time, to be sure, and he wrote even less. However, he did not neglect to look at what Vesalius and the most experienced of other authors had written about anatomy. But he taught himself in a much surer way by personally dissecting animals of different species; and he discovered directly many things more detailed than the ones that all these authors had reported in their books. For several years he continued this practice, diversifying his pursuits meanwhile through other studies. With such exactitude did he examine even the smallest parts of animal bodies that no professional physician could boast of having taken closer notice of these. He declared to Father Mersenne that after ten or eleven years of searching he had found nothing, however small, whose purpose, and whose formation through natural causes, he felt unable to explain in detail, Just as he had explained the purpose and formation of a grain of salt or a tiny snowflake in his treatise, "Les meteores." Yet after an endless number of experiments and after many year's application to studies of this kind, he was too modest to think himself able to cure even so much as a fever. His long endeavor had acquainted him only with the animal in general, and animals are not subject to fever. It was this that obliged him to apply himself thereafter more closely to the study of man, for man is subject to fever.[19]

The truth of this account of Descartes' anatomical work is seen in one of his drawings of the human brain (Figure 10), which is more accurate in its depiction of the convolutions (gyri) of the brain than those found in Vesalius' work (Figure 11). [20]

Certainly Descartes benefited from the earlier work of Vesalius, but comparison of the two figures illustrates that Descartes' own observations were, in some cases, superior to the leading anatomists of this time.[21] Furthermore, it is apparent that Descartes' work was not limited to the study of pigs.

Following this period of intense anatomical observation, Descartes was occupied with the fuller working out of his physiological ideas, as seen in a letter to the eminent priest, Guillaume Gibieuf, bearing the date of July 18, 1629, and noting, "a little treatise which I am starting," which "I hope to finish in two or three years and perhaps after that will decide to burn…for if I am not clever enough to do something well, I shall at least try to be wise enough not to publish my imperfections."[22]

Less than three years later, in a letter to Marin Hersenne, he reported progress on the work and said that it contained "a general description of the stars, the heavens, and the earth, as well as bodies on the earth." Regarding the latter, he expressed his hope to "show the way to an understanding of them through the combined use of experiment and reason."[23] Descartes entitled this work, *The World.*

Two substantial portions of *The World* survive, which he entitled *Treatise of Man* and *Treatise of Light*, both of which were written in French. A passage of unknown length and contents, connecting the two, is missing, and a third part, which would most likely have been entitled *Of the Soul,* was planned and possibly drafted.[24] Neither of the two extant parts was published during Descartes' lifetime, probably because he knew of Galileo's difficulty with the Inquisition, but he did manage to include a paraphrase of portions of the *Treatise of Man* in section V of his *Discourse on Method,* which was published anonymously in 1637.

Regarding the portion of *The World* which Descartes later entitled *Treatise of Man,* he wrote to Mersenne in the summer of 1632:

> In my *World* I shall speak somewhat more of man than I had thought to before, because I shall try to explain all his principal functions. I have already written about those that pertain to life, such as the digestion of food, the beating of the pulse, the distribution of nutrients etc., and the five senses. Now I am dissecting the heads of different animals in order to explain what imagination, memory, etc. consist of. I have seen the book *De motu cordis* of which you spoke to me earlier, and find I differ a little from his opinion which I saw only after having finished writing about this matter.[25]

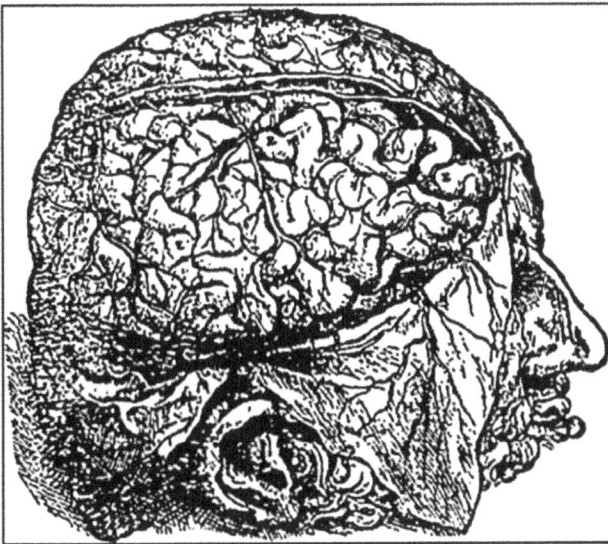

Figure 10.

From Descartes' De homine (1662)

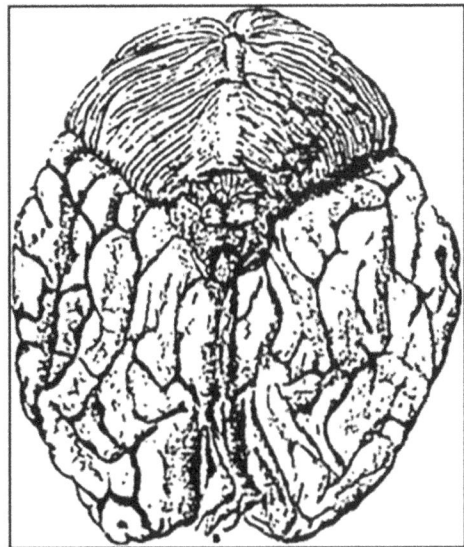

Figure 11.

From Vesalius' de fabrica (1543)

Of Descartes' Treatise of Man, Sloan writes that it "gives what William Harvey had failed to supply in the De motu cordis—an integrated physiological model on a par with that of the Galenic tradition—and has now erected this on an explicitly mechanical framework."[26]

In Descartes' description of digestion, for example, he finds only a fermentatlve process in which the particles of food are broken apart and set into agitation by fluids contained in the stomach. Chyle and excremental particles are then separated from each other in a filtration performed merely by a sieve-like configuration of the pores and vascular openings in the intestines. Chyle particles undergo yet another filtration and fermentation in the liver, where they acquire the properties of blood. Blood formed in the liver drips from the vena cava into the right ventricle of the heart, where the purely physical force of the heat of the heart quickly vaporizes the sanguinary mass. The expansion of this vapor pushes out the walls of the heart and arteries. Expansion with rarefaction is followed by cooling; and, as the vapor condenses, the heart and arteries return to their original sizes. The heart is fitted with a perfect set of valves to accommodate this process, and the man-machine described operates automatically through a system of feedback processes.

After this mechanistic survey of general physiology, Descartes moves to the nervous system, which he treats in great detail. In the man-machine described in the *Treatise,* both the automatic functioning of the human body and the lower-level cognitive functions are designed to operate without the intervention of the human will or soul.

In the next chapter, an overview of the Cartesian version of physiological psychology will be presented by exploring the complex dualistic relationship between body and soul as presented in his *Treatise,* within the context of his philosophical works.

Notes to Chapter 2

[1] D. Guglielmini, Sympos. med., sive quaestio conviv. de usu math. in arte med. (Geneva: n.p., 1719), quoted by A. Georges-Berthier, "Le Mécanisme Cartésien, et la physiologie au 17e siècle," Isis, 3 (1920), 44, translation mine.

[2] See T. S. Hall's discussion in his translation of Descartes' Treatise of Man (Cambridge: Harvard University Press, 1972), pp. xxvi-xxxiii.

[3] Hall, pp. xxvii-xxviii.

[4] Julian Jaynes, "The Problem of Animate Motion in the Seventeenth Century," Journal of the History of Ideas, 31, No. 2 (1970), 219-234.

[5] Jaynes, p. 219.

[6] See Arthur O. Lovejoy, The Great Chain of Being: A Study in the History of Ideas (Cambridge: Harvard University Press, 1936) for a discussion of the principle of plenitude.

[7] Jaynes, p. 222.

[8] Jaynes, p. 223.

[9] William Harvey, An Anatomical Disquisition on the Motion of the Heart and Blood in Animals. Trans. R. Willis. London, 1690; London: J. M. Dent & Co., 1947, pp. 56-57.

[10] J. V. de Groot, Het leven van de. H. Thomas van Aquino (Utrecht: Van Rossum, 1907), p. 141.

[11] Phillip R. Sloan, "Descartes, The Sceptics, and the Rejection of Vitalism in Seventeenth-Century Physiology," Studies in the History and Philosophy of Science, 8, No. 1 (1977), 4.

[12] Niels Stensen, "Discours sur l'Anatomie du cerveau," in Opera philosophica, ed. V. V. Maar (Copenhagen: Tryde, 1910), II, 23. Translation by Sloan, "Descartes."

[13] Jaynes, p. 220.

[14] E. J. Dijksterhuis, The Mechanization of the World Picture, trans. C. Dikshoorn (Oxford: Clarendon Press, 1961), p. 415.

[15] Descartes, p. 113.

[16] Theodore M. Brown, "Descartes: Physiology," in Dictionary of Scientific Biography (New York: Charles Scribner's Sons, 1971), IV, 61-65.

[17] Sloan, p. 4, and Brown, p. 61.

[18] Descartes, Rules for the Direction of the Mind, rule ii, in Haldane and Ross, Philosophical Works (New York: Dover, 1955), I, 3.

[19] A. Baillet, La vie de Monsieur Des-Cartes (Paris: D. Horthemels, 1691), I, 196-197, quoted in translation by I. Bernard Cohen in Foreword to T. S. Hall's trans. of Descartes' Treatise of Man, pp. xiii-xiv.

[20] Descartes, De homine (Leyden: Moyardus & Leffen, 1662), Fol. 118, Fig. Liii, reproduced in Edwin Clarke and Kenneth Dewhurst, An Illustrated History of Brain Function (Berkeley: University of California Press, 1972), Fig. 92, p. 68.

[21] Vesalius, De fabrica humani corporis (Basel, 1543), Book VII, Fig. 2, p. 607, reproduced in Clarke and Dewhurst, Fig. 82, p. 61.

[22] C. E. Adam and Paul Tannery, eds. Oeuvres de Descartes, (Paris: L. Cerf, 1897-1910), I, 17, trans. T. S. Hall, p. xxiii.

[23] Adam and Tannery, I, 243, trans. T. S. Hall, p. xxiii.

[24] See T. S. Hall's Introduction to Descartes' Treatise of Man, pp. xxiii-xxv.

[25] Adam and Tannery, I, 263, trans. T. S. Hall, p. xxiii.

CHAPTER 3:
DESCARTES' PHYSIOLOGICAL PSYCHOLOGY

Descartes' physiological psychology is based upon the foundation of a uniquely dualist ontology that attempts to define the realm of the soul, the realm of the body, and the relationship between the two. It is primarily the realm of the body that is discussed in the *Treatise of Man*, and primarily the realm of the soul that is discussed in the *Passions of the Soul*, yet sections covering the relationship between body and soul are found in both works.[1]

Descartes' *The Treatise of Man* is the best place to begin a discussion of his physiological psychology, since, as Hall notes, the work is "an essay in physiological psychology with supportive—but subordinate—sections on other physiological topics."[2] The crux of the work is to overthrow the ancient tradition which regarded soul as both (a) the motive cause of physiological function, and (b) the conscious agent of perception, volition, and reason by eliminating the physiological role altogether and by limiting the cognitive role to man.

This implicit purpose is more clearly stated in Descartes' later revision of the *Treatise*, entitled *The Description of the Human Body and All of its Functions*:

> But because it has been our experience since childhood that some of our body's movements are obedient to the will, which is a power of the soul, we have tended to believe that the soul was the cause of movements in general. To which belief the ignorance of Anatomy and Mechanics has largely contributed. For, looking only at the outside of the body, we could not imagine that there were organs enough, or force enough, within to move it in the many ways in which we see that it moves. And this error was confirmed by our suppositions that (a) dead bodies have the same organs as living from which they differ in nothing but the absence of the soul, and that (b) in dead bodies, motion is absent.
>
> But, if we try to understand our nature more clearly, we can see that, inasmuch as our soul is a substance distinct from our body, it is known to us by the simple fact that it thinks; that it, by the fact that it understands, wishes, imagines, remembers, and feels—for all these functions are varieties of thought. But other functions sometimes attributed to soul, even though they entail no thought (such as movements of the heart and arteries, digestion of food by the stomach, and the like) are merely movements of bodies. And, since bodies are ordinarily not moved by soul but rather by the movements of other bodies, such functions are more correctly attributed to the latter than the former.[4]

To eliminate the soul as the motive cause of physiological function, Descartes proposes a conceptual analogue, or model, of a man, referred to as "these men," who will form the subject of the *Treatise*:

These men will be composed, as we are, of a soul and a body; and I must first separately describe for you the body; then, also separately, the soul; and finally I must show you how these two natures would have to be joined and united to constitute men resembling us. I assume their body to be but a statue, an earthen machine formed intentionally by God to be as much as possible like us. Thus not only does He give it externally the shapes and colors of all the parts of our bodies; He also places inside it all the pieces required to make it walk, eat, breathe, and imitate whichever of our own functions can be imagined to proceed from mere matter and to depend entirely on the arrangement of our organs.

We see clocks, artificial fountains, mills, and similar machines which, though made entirely by man, lack not the power to move, of themselves, in various ways. And I think you will agree that the present machine could have even more sorts of movements, than I have imagined and more ingenuity than I have assigned, for our supposition is that it was created by God.[5]

Mechanical analogues of men and animals were familiar to Descartes, especially in articulated clock and garden figures that produced the illusion of self-instigated movement. His account of such devices is particularly descriptive (Figure 12):

Similarly you may have observed in the grottoes and fountains in the gardens of our kings that the force that makes the water leap from its source is able of itself to move divers machines and even to make them play certain instruments or pronounce certain words according to the various arrangements of the tubes through which the water is conducted.

And truly one can well compare the nerves of the machine that I am describing to the tubes of the mechanisms of these fountains, its muscles and tendons to divers other engines and springs which serve to move these mechanisms, its animal spirits to the water which drives them, of which the heart is the source and the brain's cavities the water main. Moreover, breathing and other such actions which are ordinary and natural to it, and which depend on the flow of the spirits, are like the movements of a clock or mill which the ordinary flow of water can render continuous. External objects which merely by their presence act on the organs of sense and by this means force them to move in several different ways, depending on how the parts of the brain are arranged, are like strangers who, entering some of the grottoes of these fountains, unwittingly cause the movements that then occur, since they cannot enter without stepping on certain tiles so arranged that, for example, if they approach a Diana bathing they will cause her to hide in the reeds; and if they pass farther to pursue her they will cause a Neptune to advance and menace them with his trident; or if they go in another direction they will make a marine monster come out and spew water into their faces, or other such things according to the whims of the engineers who made them. And finally when there shall be a rational soul in this machine, it will have its chief seat in the brain and will there reside like the turncock who must be in the main to which all the tubes of these machines repair when he wishes to excite, prevent, or in some manner alter their movements.[6]

The model described by Descartes is a mechanical stimulus-response device, a device which he compares with the human body, except that in the case of the human body he must further explain the nature of nerves and muscles. The account which follows is an almost totally Galenic description of the central and peripheral nervous system:

> Observe [in Fig. 13], for example, nerve A whose external membrane is like a large tube containing several other small tubes, b, c, k, l, and so on, composed of a thinner, internal membrane; and observe that these two membranes [outer and inner] are continuous with the two, K [pia] and L [dura], that envelop the brain MNO.[7]

The description maintains a continuity of nerve coats with brain coats.
As to the nature of the nerves proceeding from the brain, Descartes writes:

> Observe also that in each of the little tubes there is a sort of marrow composed of several very fine fibrils which come from the actual substance of the brain N and whose [two] extremities end, [one] at the internal surface of the cavities of the brain and, [the other] at the membranes and flesh on which the tubule containing them terminates. But because this marrow is not used to move the members, it will suffice for now that you know that it does not completely fill the tubes containing it but leaves room enough for animal spirits to flow easily through them from the brain into the muscles whither these little tubes, which should be thought of as so many little nerves, make their way.[8]

Figure 12.

Portrayal of a section of the elaborate grottoes of the royal gardens at Saint-Germain-en-Laye,
with cutaway showing hidden machinery animating classical Greek gods and goddesses

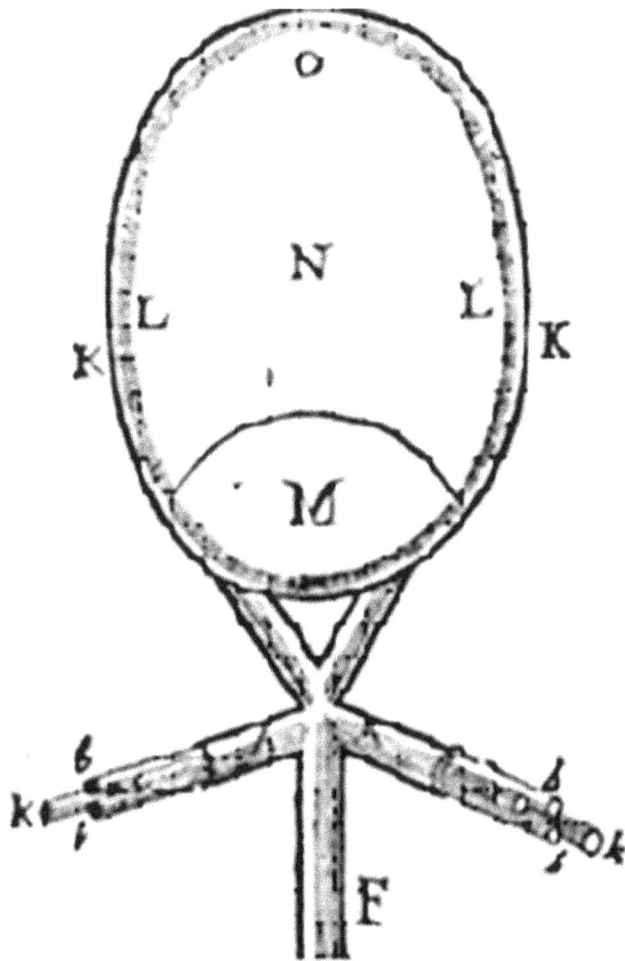

Figure 13.

Descartes' hydraulic model of the human brain

This hydraulic model attributes both sensory and motor functions to one and the same nerve, rather than what we now know are separate afferent and efferent nerves.

Descartes then addresses how the nerves are responsible for various movements of the body, via the muscular system, beginning with a description of movement of the eye:

> Next observe [in Fig. 14] how the tube or little nerve bf proceeds to muscle D, which I assume to be one of those that move the eye, and how it there divides into several branches composed of a loose membrane which can extend, enlarge, and shrink according to the quantity of animal spirits that enter or leave it, and whose branches or fibers are so arranged that when animal spirits enter therein they cause the whole body of the muscle to inflate and shorten and so pull the eye to which it is attached; while on the contrary, when they withdraw, the muscle disinflates and elongates again.[9]

He elaborates on this process in a later passage:

> For you well know that these spirits, being like a wind or a very subtle flame, cannot but flow promptly from one muscle into the other as soon as they find some passage, even though no other power propels them than that inclination which they possess to continue their movement according to the laws of nature. And you know besides that although they are very mobile and subtle, they lack not the strength to inflate and tighten the muscles in which they are enclosed, even as the air in a ball hardens it and stretches the skins that contain it.[10]

This process of hydraulic inflation of muscles is then generalized to explain other movements involved in physiological functions:

> Nor indeed is it difficult to suppose from the foregoing that the animal spirits can cause movements in all members in which nerves terminate, although there are some in which anatomists have found no nerves visible; such as the pupil of the eye, the heart, the liver, the gall bladder, the spleen, and other like organs.[11]

Thus, the process of inflation of muscles by fluids entering through nerves is assumed to be consistent throughout the body, and the mechanism responsible for movement.

After the automatic movements of blinking, breathing, and other such functions are discussed, Descartes explains movement initiated by the body's sense organs in response to stimuli external to the body:

To understand, next, how external objects that strike the sense organs can incite [the machine] to move its members in a thousand different ways, think that:

a) the filaments (I have already often told you that these come from the innermost part of the brain and compose the marrow of the nerves) are so arranged in every organ of sense that they can very easily be moved by the objects of that sense and that

b) when they are moved, with however little force, they simultaneously pull the parts of the brain from which they come, and by this means open the entrances to certain pores in the internal surface of this brain; [and that]

c) the animal spirits in its cavities begin immediately to make their way through these pores into the nerves, and so into muscles that give rise to movements in this machine quite similar to [the movements] to which we [men] are naturally incited when our senses are similarly impinged upon.[12]

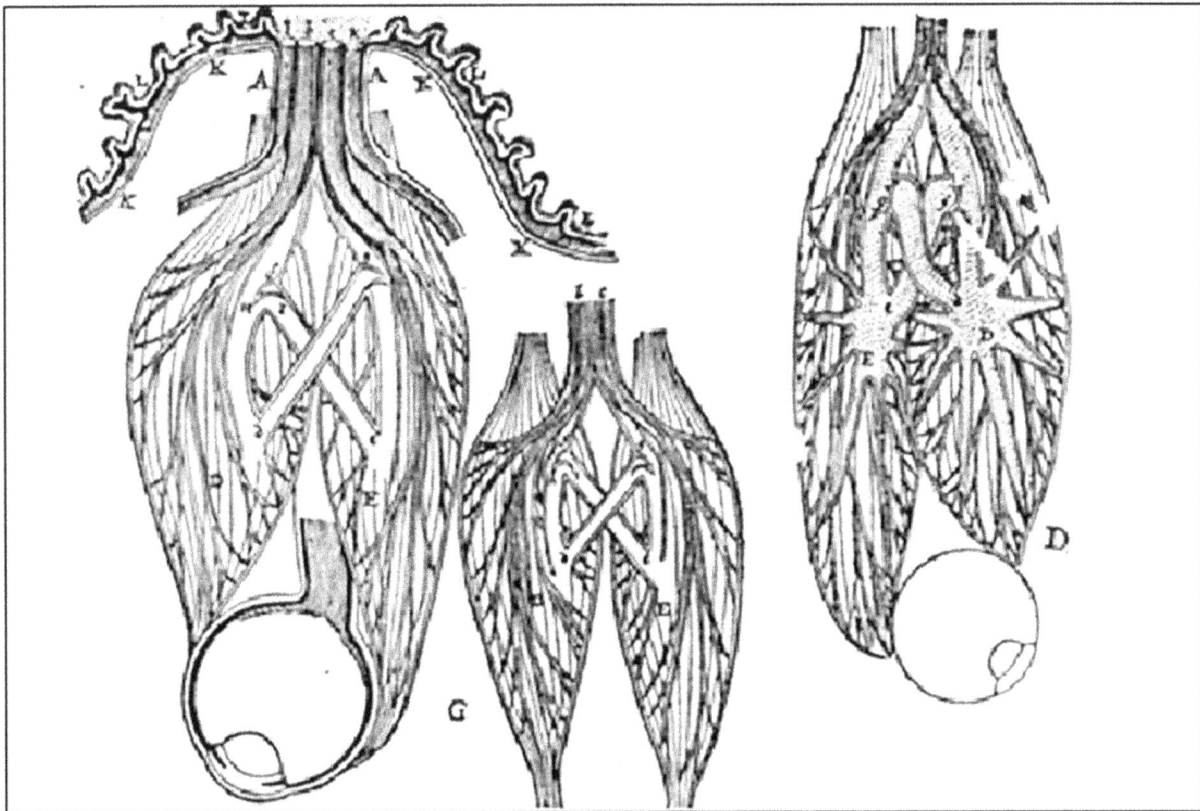

Figure 14.
Descartes' hydraulic model of eye movement.

Descartes' example of this process is noteworthy:

> Thus [in Fig. 15], if fire A is near foot B, the particles of this fire (which move very
> quickly, as you know) have force enough to displace the area of skin that they touch; and
> thus pulling the little thread cc, which you see to be attached there, they simultaneously
> open the entrance to the pore [or conduit] to where this thread terminates [in the brain]:
> just as, pulling on one end of a cord, one simultaneously rings a bell which hangs at the
> opposite end.[13]

While Descartes' description resembles what would today be seen as a reflex phenomenon—with the exception that the center for the reflex is in the spinal cord and not the brain, and that three nerves, not one, are involved—neither the term "stimulus" nor "response" is employed. As Hall notes, the process is a description of "elicitive events as well as the consequent events in the nerves, using a mechanical model."[14]

Following the description of the mechanics of automatic motions and responses to harmful stimuli, Descartes introduces the notion of the soul:

> And now I assert that when God will later join a rational soul to this machine, as I
> intend to explain further on, He will place its chief seat in the brain and will make its
> nature such that, according to the different ways in which the entrances of the pores in
> the internal surface of this brain are opened through the intervention of the nerves, the
> soul will have different feelings.[15]

Until this point in the treatise, the physiological functions have been automatic and without feeling or emotion, but the stimulus-response model of the man-machine encountering fire—a potentially painful event—introduces the possibility of conscious sensation in the automaton, a concept that Descartes reserves for the soul. The soul, according to Descartes, is the seat of feeling, emotion, ideation, and other such cognitive processes. Descartes maintains that animals are devoid of soul, and therefore exhibit only the response to harmful stimuli necessary to preserve their life, without any associated conscious perception of feeling: the response is entirely mechanical.

Since Descartes man-machine must provide a physical residence for a soul, and one that supplies the soul with useful information about the outside world, the physical basis of the soul's different feelings or emotions is next discussed. The basic principle of Descartes' theory of sensory discrimination is that different particles in motion move the outer ends of nerves in different ways, and the nerves, in turn, give rise to associated movements in the brain, which in turn are interpreted by the soul and translated into feelings or emotions:

> Thus, firstly, if the filaments that compose the marrow of these nerves are pulled with force enough to be broken and thus are separated from the part to which they were joined, so that the structure of the whole machine is somehow less intact, the movement they then cause in the brain will cause the soul (to which it is essential that its place of residence be preserved) to experience a feeling of *pain*.

And if they are pulled by a force almost as great as the preceding without, however, being broken or separated from the parts to which they are attached, they will cause a movement in the brain which, testifying to the good condition of the other parts, will cause the soul to feel a certain corporeal sensual pleasure referred to as tingling, which as you see, being very close to pain in its cause, is quite the opposite in effect.

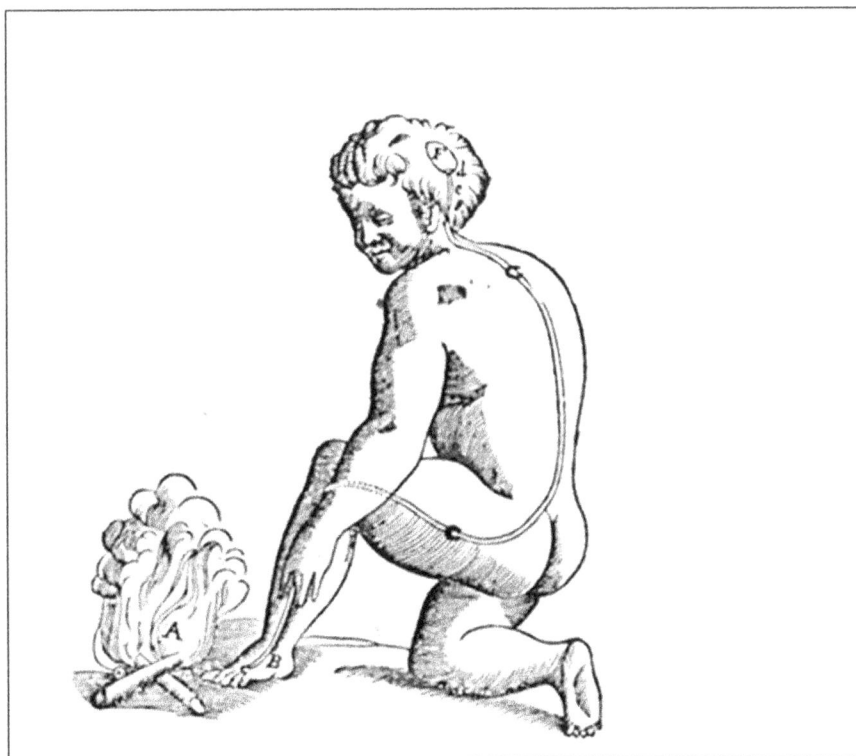

Figure 15.
Descartes' illustration of a reflex.

If many of these filaments are pulled equally and all together, they will make the soul sense that the surface of the object touching the member where they terminate is smooth; and if they are pulled unequally, they will cause the soul to feel that it is uneven and rough.

If they [the nerve filaments] are set in motion only slightly, and separately from one another, as they continually are by the heat that the heart communicates to other members, the soul will have no more sensation of this than of all other ordinary actions; but if this movement is augmented or diminished by some unusual cause, its augmentation will make the soul have a feeling of heat; its diminution, a feeling of cold. And finally, according to the divers other ways in which they are moved, they will cause [the soul] to sense all the other qualities which belong to touch in general, such as humidity, dryness, weight, and the like.

However thin and mobile these filaments may be, they are still not mobile enough to report very subtle natural events to the brain. The subtlest events they report are ones engaged in by the coarsest particles of earthy bodies. Indeed there may even be some bodies whose parts, even though coarse, will slide against the filaments so lightly that, even though they press against or even cut completely through them, their action fails to pass to the brain—just as there are certain drugs that have the power of inactivating or even corrupting the parts to which they are applied without causing us to have any sensation.[16]

Thus, Descartes accounts for feelings of pain, pleasure, texture (smoothness and roughness), humidity, weight and the like by the mechanical stimulation of nerve endings. He also accounts for stimuli falling below the threshold of sensory perception, whose associated movement of nerves "fails to pass to the brain."

Following his account of tactile phenomena, Descartes passes to a discussion of the senses of taste, smell, hearing, and vision, the last of which he covers in great detail. Each of the senses is discussed within a mechanistic framework, the notable aspect of which is the dissociation of sensations from the things that produce them, a notion so basic to Descartes' world system that the opening chapter of *The World* (or, *Treatise of Light*), an integral part of a total work including the *Treatise of Man*, is dedicated to it:

In proposing to treat here of light, the first thing I want to make clear to you is that there can be a difference between our sensation of light (i.e., the idea that is formed in our imagination through the intermediary of our eyes) and what is in the objects that produces that sensation in us (i.e., what is in the flame or in the sun that is called by the name of 'light'). For, even though everyone is commonly persuaded that the ideas that are the objects of our thought are wholly like the objects from which they proceed, nevertheless I can see no reasoning that assures us that this is the case. On the contrary, I note many experiences that should cause us to doubt it.

You well know that words bear no resemblance to the things they signify, and yet they do not cease for that reason to cause us to conceive of those things, indeed often without our paying attention to the sound of the words or to their syllables. Thus it can happen that, after having heard a discourse, the sense of which we have very well understood, we might not be able to say in what language it was uttered. Now, if words, which signify nothing except by human convention, suffice to cause us to conceive of things to which they bear no resemblance, why could not nature also have established a certain sign that would cause us to have the sensation of light, even though that sign in itself bore no similarity to that sensation? Is it not thus that she has established laughter and tears, to cause us to read joy and sorrow on the faces of men?

But perhaps you will say that our ears in fact cause us to hear only the sound of the woods, or our eyes to see only the countenance of him who laughs or cries, and that it is our mind that, having remembered what those sounds and that countenance signify, represents their meaning to us at the same time. To that I could respond that it is nonetheless our mind that represents to us the idea of light each time the action that signifies it touches our eye. But, rather than lose time in disputation, I would do better to adduce another example.

Do you think that, even when we do not pay attention to the meaning of words and hear only their sound, the idea of that sound, which forms in our thought, is anything like the object that is the cause of it? A man opens his mouth, moves his tongue, forces out his breath; in all these actions I see nothing that is not very different from the idea of the sound that they cause us to imagine.

Also, most philosophers assure us that sound is nothing other than a certain vibration of air striking against our ears. Thus, if our sense of hearing were to report to our mind the true image of its object, then, instead of causing us to conceive of sound, it would have to cause us to conceive of the motion of the parts of air that then vibrate against our ears. But, because not everyone will perhaps want to believe what the philosophers say, I will adduce another example.

Of all our senses, touch is the one thought least misleading and most certain, so that, if I show that even touch causes us to conceive many ideas that in no way resemble the objects that produce them.

I do not think you will find it strange if I say that sight can do the same. Now, there is no one who does not know that the ideas of tickling and of pain, which are formed in our thoughts when bodies from without touch us, bear no resemblance whatever to those bodies. One passes a feather lightly over the lips of a child who is falling asleep, and he perceives that someone is tickling him. Do you think the idea of tickling that he conceives resembles anything in the feather? A soldier returns from battle; during the heat of combat he could have been wounded without being aware of it. But now that he begins to cool off, he feels pain and believes he has been wounded. A surgeon is called, the soldier's armor is removed, and he is examined. In the end, one finds that what he felt was nothing but a buckler or a strap, which was caught under his armor and was pressing on him and making him uncomfortable. If, in causing him to feel this strap, his sense of touch had impressed the image on his thought, there would have been no need of a surgeon to show him what he was feeling.

Now, I see no reason forcing us to believe that what is in the objects from which the sensation of light comes to us is any more like that sensation than the actions of a feather and of a strap are like tickling and pain. Nevertheless, I have not adduced these examples to make you believe absolutely that this light is something different in the objects from what it is in our eyes, forbearing from being preoccupied by the contrary, you can now better examine with me what light is.[17]

In this passage, a thought is not a picture of the stimulus which produces it: human convention gives utterances symbolic meaning in conversation, and pleasure or pain is an index of the degree of stimulation of nerves. Descartes here lays the groundwork for a clear distinction between primary and secondary qualities, a distinction so important for the development of an experimental philosophy in the 17th century.

After discussing the five traditional "external" senses, Descartes turns to a consideration of the "internal" senses, which in Renaissance and Medieval physiological thought were generally classified as "common sense" and was some combination of "discrimination," "imagination" or "fantasy," "memory," and "reason" (see Chapter 2). To these, Descartes adds "hunger" and "thirst," and other "natural appetites" which serve to satisfy certain bodily needs.

As an example of the natural appetites, Descartes gives an explanation of the physical process eliciting the idea of hunger:

When the liquids which serve, as mentioned earlier, as a sort of *aqua fortis* in the stomach, and which enter ceaselessly from the whole mass of the blood through the extremities of the arteries, do not find there enough food to dissolve so as to employ their whole force, they turn against the stomach itself, and, agitating the filaments of its nerves more strongly than is usual, they cause motion in the parts of the brain from which the filaments come. This will cause the soul, when united to this machine, to conceive the general idea of *hunger*.[18]

To explain the physical basis of the more complex feelings or emotions, Descartes turns to a mechanical model familiar to his readers:

If you have ever had the curiosity to look closely at the organs in our churches, you know how their bellows push air into certain receptacles called—for this reason, presumably, wind trunks. [You know] also how from there the air enters the pipes, now one, now another, as the organist moves his fingers on the keyboard. And you can think of the heart and arteries of our machine (which push animal spirits into the cavities of its brain) as similar to the bellows (which push air into the wind trunks of organs); and of external objects (which, by pressing certain keys, make air from the wind trunks enter certain pipes).

Now the harmony of the organ depends not at all on the externally visible arrangement of the pipes nor on the shape of the wind trunks or other parts, but only on three things, namely [a] the air that comes from the bellows, [b] the pipes that sound, and [c] the distribution of this air to those pipes.

And let me call to your attention that, here too, the functions under consideration in no wise depend on the external shape of the visible parts which the anatomists distinguish in the substance of the brain nor on the shape of its cavities, but only [a] on the spirits that come from the heart, [b] on the pores of the brain through which they pass, and [c] on the way in which these spirits are distributed to these pores. Whence it is only necessary that I explain to you in proper order what is of most importance in connection with these three things.[19]

With this model, Descartes begins a discussion of the interrelationship between the external and internal senses, and in so doing develops a man-machine capable of interacting with its environment.

The first element of the model, the "spirits that come from the heart," is developed by a definite physical process:

The juice of the food that passes from the stomach into the veins on being mixed with the blood always communicates some of its own qualities thereto and, among other things, usually makes it more coarse when it first mixes freshly therewith. Whence, at this time, the particles of blood that the heart sends to the brain to constitute the animal spirits are generally not so agitated, strong, or abundant [as they are at other times]. Consequently they do not usually make this machine so nimble or quick as it becomes a while after digestion is finished and after the same blood, having passed and repassed through the heart several times, has become more subtle.

The air of respiration, likewise, being mixed in some way with the blood before it enters the left cavity of the heart, makes the blood kindle more strongly, and produces more lively and agitated spirits [in the heart] in dry weather than in humid weather: just as flames of every sort are found at such times to be more ardent.

When the liver is well disposed and elaborates perfectly the blood that goes to the heart, the spirits that leave this blood are correspondingly *more abundant* and more *uniformly agitated.* And should the liver happen to be incited by its nerves, the subtlest part of the blood it contains, rising directly to the heart, will produce spirits correspondingly *more abundant* and lively than is usual—though *not so uniformly agitated.*

If the gall [bladder], which is intended to purge the blood of those of its parts that are *most suited* to be enkindled in the heart, fails in its tack, or if being contracted through [the action of] its nerve it regorges into the veins the matter it contains, then the spirits will be, to that extent, *more lively and more unevenly agitated withal*.

In sum, whatever can cause any change in the blood can also cause change in the spirits. But above all, the little nerve that ends in the heart is able to dilate and contract both [a] the two entrances through which the blood of the veins and air of the lung descend, and [b] the two exits through which blood is exhaled and driven into the arteries. [Hence this nerve] can cause a thousand differences in the nature of the spirits: just as the heat of certain enclosed lamps which the alchemists use can be moderated in several ways according as one opens, to a greater or less degree, now the conduit through which the oil or other aliment of the flame comes in and now that by which the smoke goes out.[20]

Especially noteworthy in this passage is that each organ has the potential to change the nature of the animal spirits, and that the "little nerve which goes to the heart" (actually the vagus nerve) allows for psychosomatic interaction (an interaction that is actually present in vagus control of the rate of the heart beat; but not, of course, by the mechanism outlined by Descartes).

The resulting composition of the animal spirits is used by Descartes in a mechanistic version of the humoral theory of antiquity:

> Firstly, as to the animal spirits, they can be more or less *abundant*, and their part[icle]s can at different times be more or less coarse, more or less *agitated*, and more or less *uniform*; and it is by means of these four differences that all of the various humors or natural inclinations present in us are also represented in this machine (at least insofar as these do not depend on the constitution of the brain or on particular affections of the soul). For if these spirits are unusually abundant, they are appropriate for exciting movements, in this machine like movements that give evidence in us of *generosity, liberality*, and *love*. And [they excite movements that give evidence] of *confidence* or *courage* if their part[icle]s are unusually strong and coarse; and of constancy if, in addition, they are unusually uniform in shape, force, and size; and of promptness, *diligence*, and *desire* if unusually agitated; and of *tranquility of spirit* if unusually uniform in their agitation. Whereas, on the contrary, if the same qualities are lacking, these same spirits are appropriate for exciting movements in [the machine] entirely like movements in us that bear witness to *malice, timidity, inconstancy, tardiness*, and *ruthlessness*.
>
> And know that all the other humors or natural inclinations are dependent on those mentioned above. Thus the *joyous humor* is composed of promptitude and tranquility of spirit, and generosity and confidence serve to make the joyous humor more perfect. The *sad humor* is composed of tardiness and restlessness and can be augmented by malice and timidity. The *choleric humor* is composed of promptitude and restlessness, and malice and confidence fortify it. Finally, as I have just said, liberality, generosity, and love depend upon an abundance of spirits, and form in us that humor which renders us complaisant and benevolent to everyone. Curiosity and the other impulses depend upon the agitation of the part[icle]s of [the animal spirits]; and so with the other inclinations.
>
> But because these same humors or at least the passions to which they predispose us are also very dependent on the impressions that are made in the substance of the brain, you will be able to understand them better hereafter; and I shall content myself here with telling you the causes whence differences in spirits arise.[21]

In this passage, Descartes asserts that there is a correlation between the quantity and quality of animal spirits and the man-machine's *predisposition* toward certain behaviors and human characteristics, but leaves the way open for the brain to exert further control.

Descartes' description of the brain provides a central role for the pineal gland:

> Secondly, concerning the pores of the brain, they must be imagined as no different from the spaces that occur between the threads of some tissue [for example, a woven or felted fabric], because, in effect, the whole brain is nothing but a tissue constituted in a particular way, as I shall try to explain to you here.
>
> [In Figs. 16 and 17] conceive surface AA facing cavities EE to be a rather dense and compact net or mesh, all of whose links are so many little conduits which the spirits can enter and which, always facing toward gland H [the pineal] whence these spirits emanate, can easily turn hither and thither toward different points on this gland—as you see that they are turned differently in the 48th than in the 49th diagram [right and left sides of Fig. 18]. And assume that from each part of this net arise several very thin threads of which some as a rule are longer than others; and that after these threads have been differently interlaced through the space marked B, the longer of them descend toward D, and from there, comprising the marrow of the nerves, proceed to spread through all the members [see Fig. 17].
>
> Assume also that the chief characteristics of these filaments are [a] that they can be flexed rather easily in all sorts of ways merely by the force of the spirits that strike them, and [b] that they can retain, as if made of lead or wax, the flexure last received until something exerts a contrary pressure upon them.
>
> Finally, assume that the pores we are considering are nothing but the intervals between these threads and [that they] can be diversely enlarged and constricted by the force of the spirits that enter them according as that force is more or less strong and [according as the spirits] are more or less abundant; and that the shortest of these threads betake themselves to the space cc [Fig. 17], where each terminates against the extremity of one of the little vessels that are there and receives nourishment from it.[22]

This description assumes that the brain is a complex of intermeshed fibers radiating outward from the ventricles of the brain to either other parts of the brain as cranial nerves or spinal cord to the various other organs of the body. The process involved in motor control is the direction of animal spirits by the pineal gland into the proper channels for transmission to the appropriate nerve. The pineal gland is thus given the role of controlling or switching a hydraulic system which distributes the animal spirits throughout the nervous system for the performance of certain neuromuscular activities.

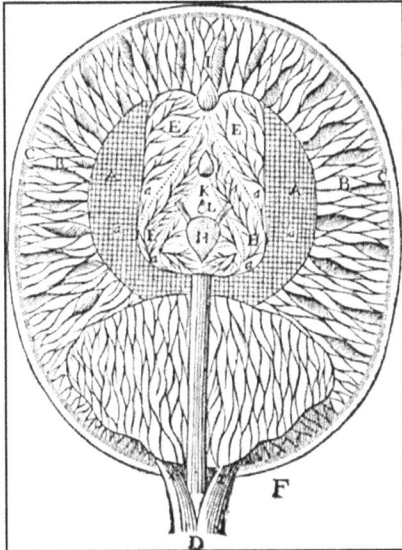

Figure 16.

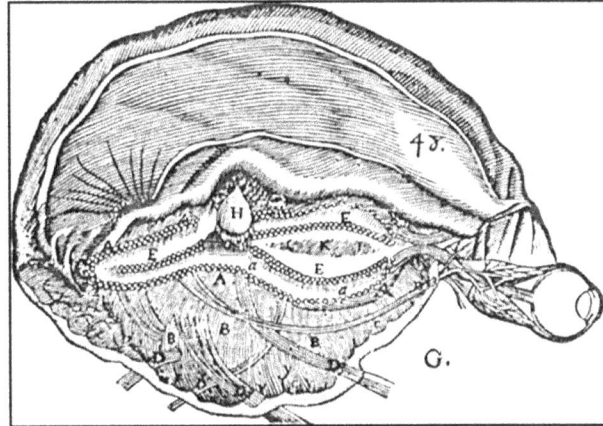

Figure 17.

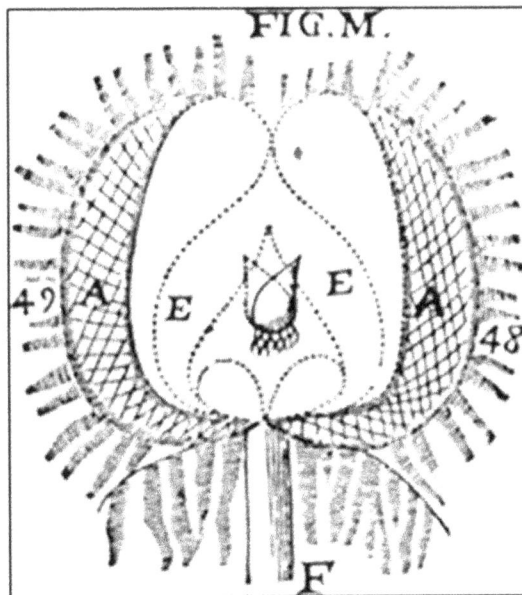

Figure 18.

A central feature of Descartes' theory of brain function is the differential flow of spirits that leave the pineal gland to move through the ventricular cavities and enter the pores of individual nerves that originate in this lining. During the waking state, a continuous, undifferentiated flow occurs, but responses to sensory input require intensified local currents which are directly linked to the stimulus itself by the following schema:

> But lest this circuitousness keep you from seeing clearly how this [mechanism] is used to form ideas of objects that impinge on the senses, notice in the adjacent drawing [Fig. 19] the filaments 1-2, 3-4, 5-6, and the like that compose the optic nerve and extend from the back of the eye (1,3,5) to the internal surface of the brain (2,4,6). Now assume that these threads are so arranged that if the rays that come, for example, from point A of the object happen to exert pressure on the back of the eye at point 1, they in this way pull the whole of thread 1-2 and enlarge the opening of the tubule marked 2. And similarly, the rays that come from point B enlarge the opening of tubule 4, and so with the others. Whence, just as the different ways in which these rays exert pressure on points 1, 3, and 5 trace a figure at the back of the eye corresponding to that of object ABC (as has already been said), so, evidently, the different ways in which tubules 2,4,6 and the like are opened by filaments 1-2, 3-4, and 5-6 must trace [a corresponding figure] on the internal surface of the brain.

Suppose next that the spirits that tend to enter each of the tubules 2,4,6, and the like do not come indifferently from all points on the surface of gland H but each from one particular point; those that come from point a of this surface, for example, tend to enter tube 2, those from points b and c tend to enter tubes 4 and 6, and so on. As a result, at the same instant that the orifices of these tubes enlarge, the spirits begin to leave the facing surfaces of the gland more freely and rapidly than they otherwise would. And [suppose] that just as [a] the different ways in which tubes 2,4, and 6 are opened trace on the internal surface of the brain a figure corresponding to that of object ABC, so [b] [the different ways] in which the spirits leave the points a, b, and c trace that figure on the surface of this gland. [23]

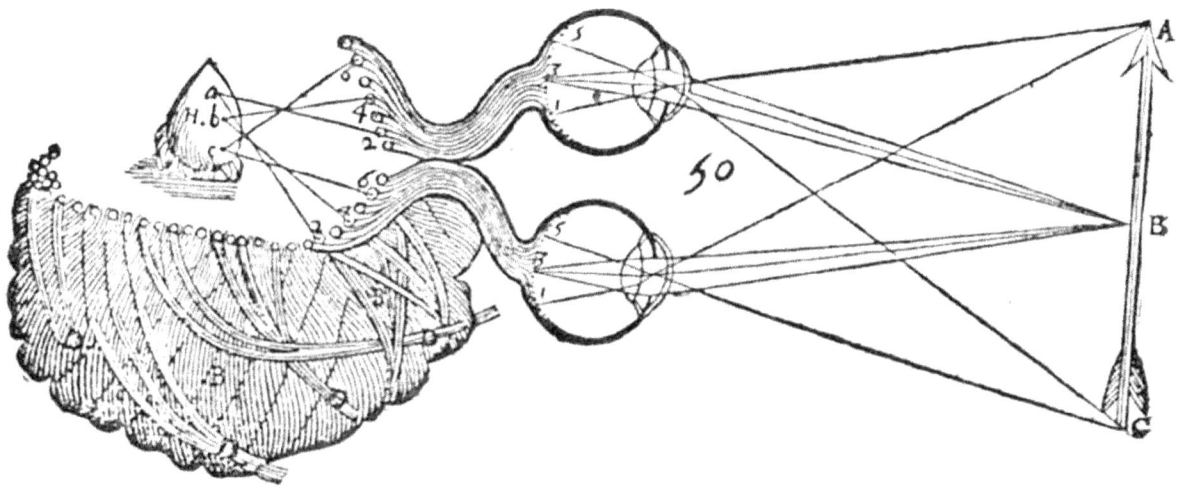

Figure 19.

What Descartes is describing is the process by which the "corpuscular particles" of light, reflected from an object, exert pressure on the retina of the eye, thereby causing the nerve endings in the retina to open in a pattern corresponding to the object itself. The open nerve endings receive animal spirits from points on the pineal gland in a direct, one-to-one correspondence. This process transfers the image of the object to the surface of the pineal.

As Hall notes, Descartes wishes to emphasize the point-to-point correspondence among four patterns: the pattern of the external object, the pattern of the retinal image, the pattern of the properties of that image on the lining of the brain cavity, and the pattern of effluence of spirits through the surface of the pineal gland. [24]

Hall also notes that, with a substitution of neuronal pathways for animal spirits, the correspondence between retinal image and cerebral pattern is generally accepted in present theories of visual perception.[25]

Descartes next explains how the objects of visual perception become "ideas":

> Now among these figures, it is not those imprinted on the organs of external sense, or on the internal surface of the brain, but only those traced in spirits on the surface of gland H, *where the seat of the imagination and common sense is*, that should be taken to be ideas, that is to say, to be the forms or images that the rational soul will consider directly when, being united to this machine, it will imagine or will sense any object.
>
> And note that I say "will imagine or will sense" inasmuch as I wish to include under the designation *Idea* all impressions that spirits receive in leaving gland H, and these [a] are all to be attributed to the common sense when they depend on the presence of objects, but [b] can also proceed from several other causes, as I shall later explain, and should be attributed to imagination.[26]

Ideas, as Descartes defines them, are "impressions" of matter received by animal spirits as they leave the pineal gland. The impression is a physical, differentiated pattern of currents, bearing a direct relationship to the external object which produced it. The fact that an "idea" can also be initiated by "imagination" will be treated in a later section.[27]

Descartes now turns to a discussion of the faculty of memory:

> But I shall content myself with telling you more about how they [ideas] are imprinted in the internal part of the brain, marked B, which is the seat of *Memory*.
>
> With this end in view, imagine that after leaving gland H [see Fig. 19] spirits pass through tubes 2,4,6 and the like, and into the pores or intervals that occur between the

filaments composing part [the solid part] of the brain. And [assume] that they are forceful enough to enlarge these intervals somewhat and to bend and rearrange any filaments they encounter, according to the differing modes of movement of the spirits themselves and the differing degrees of openness of the tubes into which they pass. [Assume also] that the first time they accomplish this they do so less easily and effectively here than on gland H, but that they accomplish it increasingly effectively in the measure that their action is stronger, or lasts longer, or is more often repeated. Which is why in such cases these patterns are no longer so easily erased, but are retained there in such a way that by means of them the ideas that existed previously on this gland can be formed again long afterward, without requiring the presence of the objects to which they correspond. And it is in that Memory consists.[27]

As an example of this process, Descartes compares the impressions made on the brain with impressions made by needles passed through a linen cloth [Fig. 20]. The point being made is that the holes in the cloth remain after the needles are withdrawn.

Descartes next discusses the relationship between the brain and the pineal gland:

> Consider furthermore that gland H is composed of matter which is very soft and that it is not completely joined and united to the substance of the brain but only attached to certain little arteries whose membranes are rather lax and pliant, and that it is sustained as if in balance by the force of the blood which the heat of the heart pushes thither. [And suppose that] therefore very little [force] is required to cause it to incline and to lean, now more now less, now to this side now to that, and so to dispose the spirits that leave and make their way toward certain regions of the brain rather than toward others.[29]

To produce a particular bodily movement, the pineal gland must direct spirits from a specific part of itself into the appropriate nerve tubules, a process that depends upon its leaning in a definite direction. This leaning, Descartes notes, depends upon two principal causes, not counting the force of the soul: 1) differences among the particles of the spirits that leave the pineal gland, and 2) the action of objects that impinge upon the senses.

Regarding the differences in the particles of the spirits that leave the gland, Descartes discusses two effects:

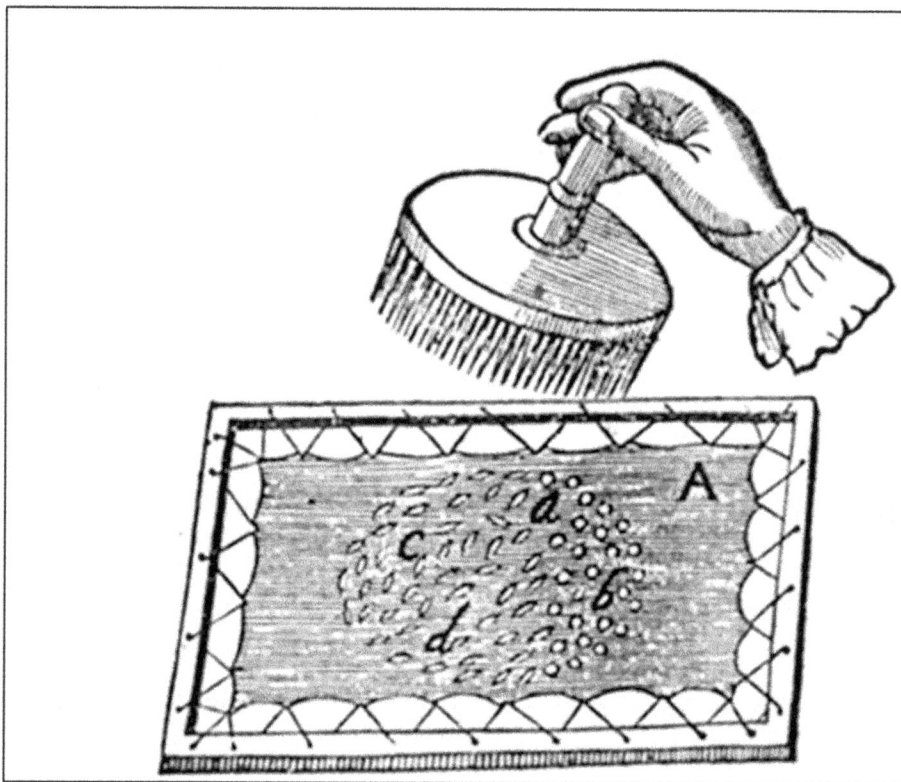

Figure 20.

Now the chief effect that follows from this is that the spirits, departing from certain regions on the surface of this gland and not from others, have force enough [to do two things]: [1] They can turn the tubules into which they flow, in the inner brain surface, toward the places where these spirits emanate from the gland (u)

less the tubules in question are already pointed in that direction). And [2] they can make the members to which these tubules correspond turn toward places corresponding to the indicated regions on the surface of gland H. And note that if we have an idea about moving a member, that idea—consisting of nothing but the way in which spirits flow from the gland—is the cause of the movement itself.[30] Now the chief effect that follows from this is that the spirits, departing from certain regions on the surface of this gland and not from others, have force enough [to do two things]: [1] They can turn the tubules into which they flow, in the inner brain surface, toward the places where these spirits emanate from the gland (unless the tubules in question are already pointed in that direction; and [2] they can make the members to which these tubules correspond turn toward places corresponding to the indicated regions on the surface of gland H. And note that if we have an idea about moving a member, that idea—consisting of nothing but the way in which spirits flow from the gland—is the cause of the movement itself.[30]

Ideas, materially defined as the differential flow patterns assumed by spirits leaving the pineal gland, can thus initiate involuntary movements of the body in which the soul—and therefore consciousness—plays no role. Thus, Descartes' account of the man-machine allows for what would today be called subconscious behavior.

Next, Descartes notes that ideas (again defined as the differential flow pattern of spirits leaving the pineal gland) can also be formed by memories:

It remains to be noted that when gland H is inclined in one direction by the force of the spirits alone, without the aid of the rational soul or of the external senses, the ideas that are formed on its surface proceed not only [a] from inequalities in the particles of the spirits causing corresponding differences in temper, as mentioned before but also [b] from the imprints of memory.

For if at the region of the brain toward which the gland is inclined, the shape of one particular object is imprinted more distinctly than that of any other, the spirits tending to that region cannot fail to receive an impression thereof.

And it is thus that past things sometimes return to thought as if by chance and without the memory of them being excited by any object impinging on the senses.[31]

After discussing the effect of the difference in the nature of the spirits upon the movement of that gland, Descartes turns to a consideration of the effect of objects which impinge upon the senses:

> The second cause which can determine the movements of gland H is the action of objects that impinge on the senses. For it is easy to understand [see Fig. 21] that when the degree of openness of tubules 2,4, and 6, for example, is increased by the action of object ABC, the spirits, which commence at once to flow toward them more freely and rapidly than they did [before], draw the gland after themselves a little, and cause it to lean if it is not otherwise prevented from so doing; so that, changing the position of its pires, it begins to conduct a much greater quantity of spirits through a, b, and c to 2, 4, and 6 than it did before: which renders the idea that these spirits form correspondingly more perfect. This constitutes the first effect that I wish you to notice.
>
> The second consists in [the fact] that while leaning thus to one side this gland is prevented from easily receiving ideas of objects acting on other sense organs. For example, [see Fig. 21] during the time when almost all the spirits that gland H produces leave it from points a, b, and c, too few leave from point d to form there the idea of object D whose action I assume to be neither as lively nor as strong as that of object ABC. Whence you see how ideas mutually impede one another and why one cannot be strongly attentive to several things at one time.[32]

In addition to the effect of objects of sensory perception on movements of the pineal, Descartes allows for selective discrimination of sensory phenomena, an action actually performed in the thalamus of the brainstem.

The exact mechanism whereby the object of sensory impression affects the pineal is then outlined:

> It thus only remains for me to tell you what cause can thus initiate the movement of the gland.
>
> This is ordinarily nothing but the force of the object itself which, acting on a sense organ, augments the openness of certain of the tubules in the internal surface of the brain, so that spirits, beginning promptly to flow toward these tubules, draw the gland with them and make it lean in that direction. But in case the tubes on this side have already been otherwise opened to the same or a greater extent than this object would open them, we must suppose that the spirit particles flowing out in every direction through the pores of the gland, being unequal, will push the gland hither and thither in

the twinkling of an eye without giving it a moment's respite. And if they should happen first to push it in a direction in which it is not easily inclined [because the pores on that side are not open very wide] their action, being in itself rather slight, will have very little effect. But as soon as they push it ever so slightly in the direction in which it is already carried [by the already widely opened pores], it will not fail to lean that way promptly and, as a result, to dispose the sense organ to receive the action of its object in the most perfect possible way, as just explained.[33]

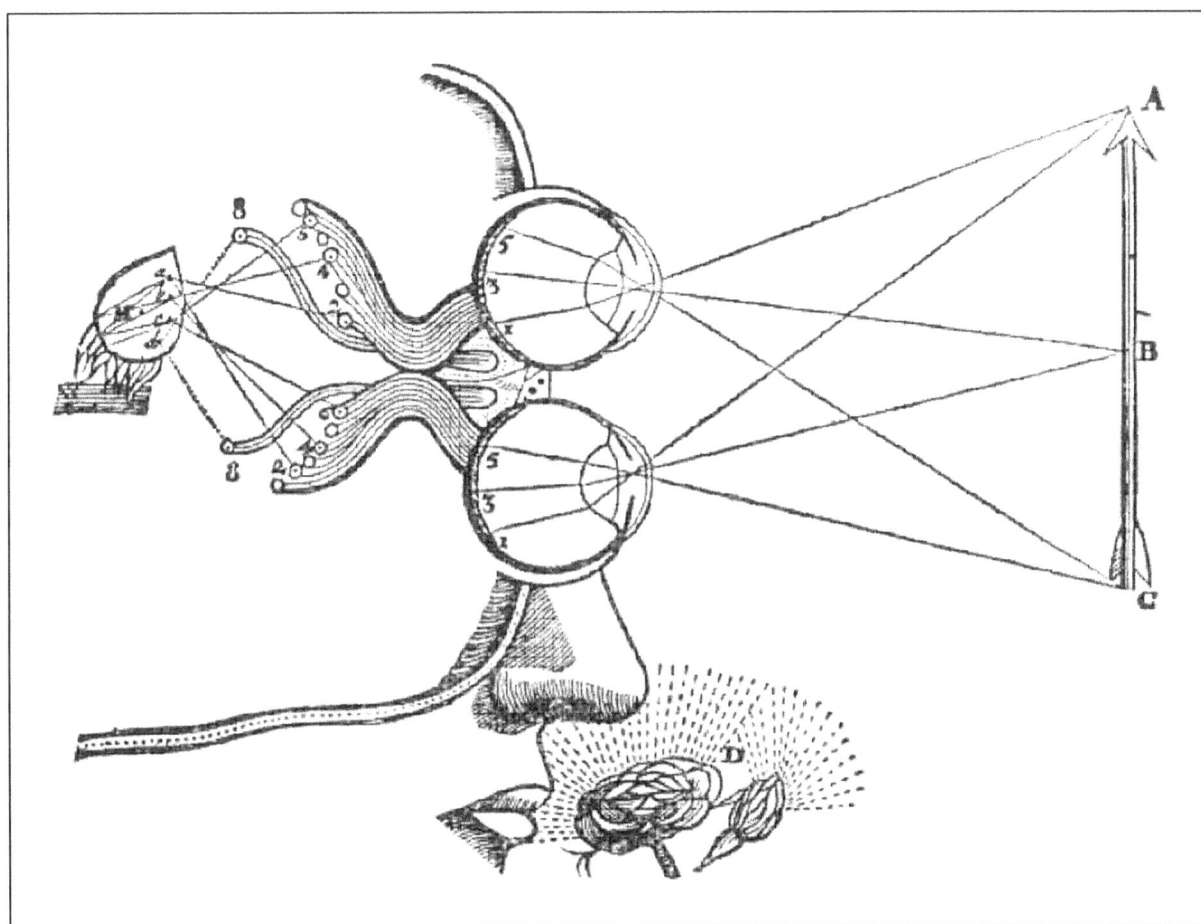

Figure 21.

Descartes is describing a process of what would today be called facilitation, in which a single neurological stimulation increases the efficacy of a subsequent stimulation by paving the way for it. In Descartes' model, objects of the senses are more readily and clearly interpreted if the movement of the pineal gland is in a certain direction, a direction determined by a focusing of attention on the object. In other words, if the pineal is leaning in a certain direction, certain senses are facilitated.

Next, Descartes describes how the sensory impressions, by causing a movement of the pineal, are responsible for an associated bodily movement:

> Let us have done with conducting the spirits to the nerves, and see now what movements depend on them. Suppose that none of the tubules of the internal surface of the brain are more open than any others, and that consequently the spirits have no impression in them of any particular idea. [In such a case] they [the spirits] will spread indifferently in all directions and pass from the conduits which are near B [the deeper regions of the brain mass] and into those near C [the superficial regions of the brain mass], whence the most subtle of their parts flow off directly from the brain through the pores of the little membrane which envelopes it [the pia mater] while the rest, making their way toward D, will proceed into the nerves, and thence into the muscles, without causing there any particular effect because they will be distributed to all muscles equally.
>
> But if by the action of the objects that move our senses, some tubules are more or less opened—or even just differently opened--than others, the filaments that compose the brain substance being consequently some a little more tense or more slack than others, will conduct the spirits toward certain regions near its base and thence toward certain nerves with more or less force than toward others. Which will suffice to cause different movements in the muscles, in accordance with what has already been amply explained.[34]

Descartes proceeds to develop a more detailed theory of automatic responses to given sensory stimuli than he has presented thus far. His explanation proposes, in considerable detail, a correlation of the qualities of the objects of the senses and the different kinds of brain responses they evoke. When Descartes says that different qualities open the tubules "more or less," or "just differently," he means that the recipient orifices in the brain lining can be variously oriented as well as opened in differing degrees. The result of this process will be corresponding differences in the pattern of spirits entering these orifices, and consequently in the differential displacement of the filaments in the brain.

Regarding the arrangement of the filaments in the brain, Descartes notes two types, "natural" or "acquired:"

As to the arrangement of the filaments that compose the brain substance, it is either acquired or natural [innate]; and since acquired arrangements depend on circumstances that change the flow of the spirits, I shall be better able to explain them later on. First, then, to explain what the natural arrangements consist in. Know that in forming the filaments God arranged them as follows. The passages that He left among them are able to conduct the spirits, when these are moved by a particular stimulant action, toward nerves that permit just those movements in this machine that a similar action could incite in us when we act through natural instincts.[35]

Hall notes that "ancient and medieval authors acknowledged that the body contains both a predisposition and an ability to give complex automatic (unlearned) responses, that is, to behave in a manner which would later be termed 'instinctive'."[36] Viewed in terms of reflex behavior, certain responses are "built in" (spinal and medullary reflexes), and others are acquired by conditioning (stimulus-response). As such, Descartes' man-machine is capable of certain feats of "learning," but discussion of this aspect of the model does not appear in the *Treatise of Man*. Such conditioned reflexes are discussed, however, in his *Passions of the Soul*.

Descartes defines "passions" as follows:

Passions serve to dispose the heart, the liver, and all the other organs that determine the temperament of blood—and consequently of spirits—in such a way that the spirits formed at a given time will be those suited for producing the external movements that follow.[37]

Descartes' treatment of the passions is very brief in the *Treatise of Man*, since they are mentioned only in connection with a certain predisposition of the man-machine toward certain behavior. A fuller and more complete discussion is saved for his later treatise, *The Passions of the Soul*.

Descartes next discusses volition, or the conscious instigation of muscular motion:

Similarly, to understand how a single action can, without changing, move first one foot of this machine and then the other, as is required for it to walk, it suffices to suppose that the spirits pass through a single conduit [in the brain lining], a conduit whose extremity [that is, whose inner orifice] is differently disposed—and so conducts them into different nerves—when the left foot is advanced than when the right is. And relatable to this is all that I have said hitherto concerning respiration and such other movements as do not ordinarily depend on any idea [that is, reflexes]; I say ordinarily, because they can also depend upon them at times.[38]

In Descartes' model, volition begins with ideas which, as explained earlier, are currents in the spirits contained within the ventricles of the brain, created as the spirits enter from the pineal gland. In the foregoing passage, Descartes discusses the currents caused by conscious command; the results, in short of the soul's determination of which pores on the surface of the pineal gland the spirits will enter. Descartes leaves the way open for conscious control of certain (normally) automatic reflexes, such as breathing.

The last aspect of the man-machine discussed by Descartes is the subject of the two major states of the brain: waking and sleeping. Descartes' theory is, basically, that exhaustion of spirits in a waking person induces the brain to enter the sleeping state. The sleeping state differs from the waking state in that the fibers in the brain are in a greater state of tension in the waking than in the sleeping state.

Descartes' summary statements leading into the final paragraphs of the *Treatise of Man* might well serve as an introduction to his later work, *The Passions of the Soul*:

> But before I pass to the description of the rational soul, I still wish you to reflect a little on all that I have just said about this machine; and to consider, firstly, that I have supposed in it only such organs and springs of power as may easily persuade you that wholly similar ones are present both in us and in many nonrational animals as well.[39]

Descartes' original plan, as noted in the opening paragraph of the *Treatise*, had been to discuss the body first, then the soul, and then their interactions; but this plan was not to be completed in the *Treatise*. The first part of the tripartite plan was achieved in that Descartes described the body without relying upon a physiological role for the soul. The remaining two parts, however, were never completed as part of the *Treatise of Man,* but were to be treated many years later in his work The *Passions of the Soul*, where he limited the cognitive role of the soul to man.

Before beginning a discussion of The *Passions of the Soul*, it should be noted that all behavior described in the man-machine of the *Treatise of Man* is at the unconscious or pre-conscious level. Descartes' man-machine is, in effect, a lobotomized patient.

Turning to Descartes' *The Passions of the Soul*, a review of articles I through XVI reveals that this section of the work is a recapitulation of the *Treatise of Man*, after which a discussion of the soul ensues:

> After having thus considered all the functions which pertain to the body alone, it is easy to recognize that there is nothing in us which we ought to attribute to our soul excepting our thoughts, which are mainly of two sorts, the one being the actions of the soul, and the other its passions. Those which I call its actions are all our desires, because

we find by experience that they proceed directly from our soul, and appear to depend on it alone; while, on the other hand, we may usually term one's passions all those kinds of perception or forms of knowledge which are found in us, because it is often not our soul which makes them what they are, and because it always receives them from the things which are represented by them.[40]

Descartes' discussion of the nature of the soul begins with a distinction between "actions" and "passions" of the soul. "Passions" differ from "actions" of the soul by depending upon a corporal, bodily mechanism rather than upon the direct action of the soul. An act of will, for example, would be an action of the soul, whereas emotional states are considered passions of the soul:

> After having considered in what the passions of the soul differ from all its other thoughts, it seems to me that we may define them generally as the perceptions, feelings, or emotions of the soul which we relate specially to it, and which are caused, maintained, and fortified by some movement of the spirits.[41]

Having defined the passions of the soul, explaining that they depend upon the animal spirits, Descartes describes the location of the seat of the soul:

> It is likewise necessary to know that although the soul is joined to the whole body, there is yet in that a certain part in which it exercises its functions more particularly than in all the others; and it is usually believed that this part is the brain, or possibly the heart: the brain, because it is with it that the organs of sense are connected, and the heart because it is apparently in it that we experience the passions. But, in examining the matter with care, it seems as though I had clearly ascertained that the part of the body in which the soul exercises its functions immediately is in nowise the heart, nor the whole of the brain, but merely the most inward of all its parts, to wit, a certain very small gland which is situated in the middle of its substance and so suspended above the duct whereby the animal spirits in its anterior cavities have communication with those in the posterior, that the slightest movements which take place in it may later vary greatly the course of these spirits; and reciprocally that the smallest changes which occur in the course of the spirits may, do much to change the movements of this gland.[42]

Descartes' logic for locating the principal site of activity of the soul in the pineal gland follows:

> The reason which persuades me that the soul cannot have any other seat in all the
> body than this gland wherein to exercise its functions immediately, is that l reflect that
> the other parts of our brain are all of them double, just as we have two eyes, two hands,
> two ears, and finally all the organs of our outside senses are double; and inasmuch as we
> have but one solitary and simple thought of one particular thing at one and the same
> moment, it must necessarily be the case that there must somewhere be a place where the
> two images which come to us by the two eyes, where the two other impressions which
> proceed from a single object by means of the double organs of the other senses, can unite
> before arriving at the soul, in order that they may not represent to it two objects instead
> of one. And it is easy to apprehend how these images or other impressions might unite
> in this gland by the intermission of the spirits which fill the cavities of the brain: but
> there is no other place in the body where they can be thus united unless they are so in
> this gland.[43]

Descartes' argument follows his rules of scientific evidence set forth in his earlier *Discourse on the
Method* in that it is clear and distinct—at least from the standpoint of a hypothetical model. From the
argument of the pineal gland being the only single or non-paired part of the brain, the hypothalamus
could just as easily have been chosen; but from the additional requirement of proximity to the flow of
spirits in the brain (as described in the man-machine of *The Treatise of Man*), the pineal gland was the
organ of choice.

After locating the principal activity of the soul in the pineal gland, Descartes discusses the nature of
the interaction between the soul and the body:

> Let us then conceive here that the soul has its principal seat in the little gland which
> exists in the middle of the brain, from whence it radiates forth through all the remainder
> of the body by means of the animal spirits, nerves, and even the blood, which,
> participating in the impressions of the spirits, can carry them by the arteries into all the
> members. And recollecting what has been said above about the machine of our body, i.e.
> that the little filaments of our nerves are so distributed in all its parts, that on the
> occasion of the diverse movements which are there excited by sensible objects, they open
> in diverse ways the pores of the brain, which causes the animal spirits contained in these
> cavities to enter in diverse ways into the muscles, by which means they can move the
> members in all the different ways in which they are capable of being moved; and also
> that all the other causes which are capable of moving the spirits in diverse ways suffice to

conduct them into diverse muscles; let us here add that the small gland which is the main seat of the soul is so suspended between the cavities which contain the spirits that it can be moved by them in as many different ways as there are sensible diversities in the object, but that it may also be moved in diverse ways by the soul, whose nature is such that it receives in itself as many diverse impressions, that is to say, that it possesses as many diverse perceptions as there are diverse movements in this gland. Reciprocally, likewise, the machine of the body is so formed that from the single fact that this gland is diversely moved by the soul, or by such other cause, whatever it is, it thrusts the spirits which surround it towards the pores of the brain, which conduct them by the nerves into the muscles, by which means it causes them to move the limbs.[44]

The important part of this description is that the pineal gland is the site of interaction between the soul, the passions, and sensory input in the form of "ideas" as previously described in the *Treatise of Man*. As such, the pineal gland is seen as a sensory integration center, playing the role actually performed by the thalamus of the brain.

Next, Descartes gives an example of how the passions are excited in the soul:

And, besides that, if this figure is very strange and frightful—that is, if it has a close relationship with the things which have been formerly hurtful to the body, that excites the passion of apprehension in the soul and then that of courage, or else that of fear and consternation according to the particular temperament of the body or the strength of the soul, and according as we have to begin with been secured by defence or by flight against the hurtful things to which the present impression is related. For in certain persons that disposes the brain in such a way that the spirits reflected from the image thus formed on the gland, proceed thence to take their places partly in the nerves which serve to turn the back and dispose the legs for flight, and partly in those which so increase or diminish the orifices of the heart, or at least which so agitate the other parts from whence the blood is sent to it, that this blood being there rarefied in a different manner from usual, sends to the brain the spirits which are adapted for the maintenance and strengthening of the passion of fear; i.e. which are adapted to the holding open, or at least reopening, of the pores of the brain which conduct them into the same nerves. For from the fact alone that these spirits enter into these pores, they excite a particular movement in this gland which is instituted by nature in order to cause the soul to be sensible of this passion; and because these pores are principally in relation with the little nerves which serve to contract or enlarge the orifices of the heart, that causes the soul to be sensible of it for the most part as in the heart.[45]

Descartes' description of the body's response to a potentially harmful stimulus is strikingly similar to what is now known as the "fight or flight" response, attributed to the famous 19th century physiologist, W. B. Cannon. Moreover, Descartes' description allows for previous encounters with the object, during which the body has been conditioned to avoid a harmful stimulus. The description of the actual interaction between the soul and the pineal gland is, however, vague.

Descartes further asserts that passions may be initiated entirely by the body, and yet not sensed by the soul:

> For the rest, in the same way as the course which these spirits take towards the nerves of the heart suffices to give the movement to the gland by which fear is placed in the soul, so, too, by the simple fact that certain spirits at the same time proceed towards the nerves which serve to move the legs in order to take flight, they cause another movement in the same gland, by means of which the soul is sensible of and perceives this flight, which in this way may be excited in the body by the disposition of the organs alone, and without the soul's contributing thereto.[46]

Thus, the body can cause a self-preserving action independent of the soul's direction when the soul chooses not to intervene.

The principal use of the passions is next described:

> For it is requisite to notice that the principal effect of all the passions in men is that they incite and dispose their soul to desire those things for which they prepare their body, so that the feeling of fear incites it to desire to fly that of courage to desire to fight, and so on.[47]

The passions, according to Descartes, serve a role of self-preservation, predisposing the body to undertake action in its best interest.

After describing the physical nature of the passions, Descartes turns to a consideration of the power that the soul can exert over the body:

> And the whole action of the soul consists in this, that solely because it desires something, it causes the little gland to which it is closely united to move in the way requisite to produce the effect which relates to this desire.[48]

Descartes has succeeded in banishing the soul from its ancient role of animating living bodies only to reappoint it as the sovereign of the higher cognitive faculties.

In the remainder of Part I of *The Passions of the Soul*, Descartes explains how the soul, acting in some mysterious manner, accomplishes its will through the intermediary of the pineal gland. Memory, for example, operates by the same mechanism as described in the *Treatise of Man*, but may be activated upon command by the soul:

> Thus when the soul desires to recollect something, this desire causes the gland, by inclining successively to different sides, to thrust the spirits towards different parts of the brain until they come across that part where the traces left there by the object which we wish to recollect are found; for these traces are none other than the fact that the pores of the brain, by which the spirits have formerly followed their course because of the presence of this object, have by that means acquired a greater facility than the others in being once more opened by the animal spirits which come towards them in the same way. Thus these spirits in coming in contact with these pores, enter into them more easily than into the others, by which means they excite a special movement in the gland which represents the same object to the soul, and causes it to know that it is this which it desired to remember.[49]

The action of the soul is totally unexplained—simply by willing an act, the soul achieves its effect.

But since the "natural appetites" or baser passions can also act on the pineal gland, there is sometimes reason for strife:

> And it is only in the repugnance which exists between the movements which the body by its animal spirits, and the soul by its will, tend to excite in the gland at the same time, that all the strife which we are in the habit of conceiving to exist between the inferior part of the soul, which we call the sensuous, and the superior, which is rational, or as we may say, between the natural appetites and the will, consists. For there is within us but one soul, and this soul has not in itself any diversity of parts; the same part that is subject to sense impressions is rational, and all the soul's appetites are acts of will. The error which has been committed in making it play the part of various personages, usually in opposition one to another, only proceeds from the fact that we have not properly distinguished its functions from those of the body, to which alone we must attribute everything which can be observed in us that is opposed to our reason; so that there is here no strife, excepting that the small gland which exists in the middle of the

brain, being capable of being thrust to one side by the soul, and to the other by the animal spirits, which are mere bodies, as I have said above, it often happens that these two impulses are contrary, and that the stronger prevents the other from taking effect.[50]

Mankind's departure from perfect acts of reason is not, then, to be attributed to a baser part of the soul, but to the bodily desires which are in conflict with the soul. Thus the battleground between the soul and the body is to be found in the pineal gland, where a tug-of-war is played out for control of the individual.

Numerous psychological states are explained in *The Passions of the Soul*, all within the context of between the will, the passions, and the pineal gland, the most interesting of which is his account of innate and conditioned behavior:

> And it is useful here to know that, as has already been said above, although each movement of the gland seems to have been joined by nature to each one of our thoughts from the beginning of our life, we may at the same time join them to others by means of custom, as experience shows us in the case of words which excite movements in the gland, which, so far as the institution of nature is concerned, do not represent to the soul more than their sound when they are uttered by the voice, or the form of their letters when they are written, and which, nevertheless, by the custom which has been acquired in thinking of what they signify when their sound has been heard or their letters have been seen, usually make this signification to be understood rather than the form of their letters or the sound of their syllables. It is also useful to know that although the movements both of the gland and of the spirits of the brain, which represent certain objects to the soul, are naturally joined to those which excite in it certain passions, they can at the same time be separated from these by custom, and joined to others which are very different; and also that this custom can be acquired by a solitary action, and does not require long usage. Thus when we unexpectedly meet with something very foul in food that we are eating with relish, the surprise that this event gives us may so change the disposition of our brain, that we can no longer see any such food without horror, while we formerly ate it with pleasure. And the same thing is to be noticed in brutes, for although they have no reason, nor perhaps any thought, all the movements of the spirits and of the gland which excite the passions in us, are none the less in them, and in them serve in maintaining and strengthening not, as in our case, the passions, but the movements of the nerve and muscles which usually accompany them. So when a dog sees a partridge he is naturally disposed to run towards it, and when he hears a gun fired,

this sound naturally incites him to flight. But nevertheless setters are usually so trained that the sight of a partridge causes them to stop, and the sound which they afterwards hear when a shot is fired over them, causes them to run up to us. And these things are useful in inciting each one of us to study to regard our passions; for since we can with a little industry change the movement of the brain in animals deprived of reason, it is evident that we can do so yet more in the case of men, and that even those who have the feeblest souls can acquire a very absolute dominion over their passions if sufficient industry is applied in training and guiding them.[51]

In short, Pavlov's dogs find their precursors in Descartes' setters.

In Part II of *The Passions of the Soul*, Descartes enumerates and explains the six primitive passions—wonder, love, hatred, desire, joy, and sadness—of which a host of other complex passions are constituted. However complex the passions, their elemental or primitive form is simple and material in nature:

> We know from what has been said above that the ultimate and most proximate cause of the passions of the soul is none other than the agitation with which the spirits move the little gland which is in the middle of the brain.[52]

Consequently, the passions are no more than physical inclinations caused by the action of the animal spirits upon the pineal gland, responsible for affecting, but not controlling, behavior.

Toward the end of Part II of *The Passions of the Soul*, Descartes introduces a distinction between the passions of the soul and what he chooses to call the "interior emotions of the soul:

> I shall only add here a consideration which, it seems to me, we shall find of much service in preventing us from suffering any inconvenience from the passions; and that is that our good and our harm depend mainly on the interior emotions which are only excited in the soul by the soul itself, in which respect they differ from its passions, which always depend on some movement of the spirits. And, although these emotions of the soul are frequently united to the passions which are similar to them, they may likewise often be met with along with others, and even take their origin from those which are contrary to them. For example, when a husband laments his dead wife whom (as sometimes happens) he would be sorry to see brought to life again, it may be that his heart is oppressed by the sadness that the appurtenances of woe and the absence of one to whose conversation he was used excite in him; and it may be that some remnants of

love or pity which present themselves to his imagination draw sincere tears from his eyes, notwithstanding that he yet feels a secret joy in the inmost parts of his heart, the emotion of which possesses so much power that the sadness and the tears which accompany it can do nothing to diminish its force. And when we read of strange adventures in a book, or see them represented in a theatre, which sometimes excite sadness in us, sometimes joy, or love, or hatred, and generally speaking all the passions, according to the diversity of the objects which are offered to our imagination; but along with that we have pleasure in feeling them excited in us, and this pleasure is an intellectual joy which may as easily take its origin from sadness as from any of the other passions.[53]

This is a curious passage since Descartes does not elaborate further on the interior emotions of the soul. In any event, Descartes recognized the complexity of certain human feelings and made allowances for paradoxical states of mind by reserving a category of undefined emotions for the soul alone.

Since Part III of *The Passions of the Soul* elaborates upon individual complex passions which have no bearing upon this study, this section of the work will not be discussed.

The underlying premise in Descartes' *Treatise of Man* and *The Passions of the Soul* is that most human motions (such as digestion, heartbeat, reflex responses, and other functions not controlled by conscious action) do not depend upon the mind, but are strictly mechanistic. His doctrine that animals are pure machines while men are machines with minds was probably a compromise between his scientific and religious views of man. Descartes was actually working within the sensitive area of religious issues when he passed from a mechanistic account of biological function in the *Treatise of Man* to an explanation of the soul's function in The *Passions of the Soul.* The debates which surrounded soul or mind were then, as now, sensitive indicators of fundamental issues in philosophy and science: the immortality of the soul, the immateriality of the human mind, and the basis of free will and responsibility.

While the application of mechanism to animals and to the human body had considerable utility as an alternative to animistic or psychistic explanations in physiology, the demands of functional explanation in biology made Descartes' description of the interaction between soul and body through the pineal gland ultimately untenable.

The future of science demanded a continuity between animals and man that 17th century metaphysics and theology denied. The transition from animal-machine to man-machine was never completely made by Descartes, but his hypothetical model of man served the broader purpose of a biological model which allowed future scientists a non-psychistic explanation of life phenomena.

Notes to Chapter 3

[1] Descartes' major writings in physiology are the *Dioptrics* (published in 1637 as one of the three works to which the *Discourse* was published as an introduction; treats the eye and the general subject of sensation), *Description of the Human Body* (published 1664). Descartes suppressed the *Treatise of Light* during his life-time because of Galileo's problems with the Church over the Copernican doctrine which were "so connected with every other part of my Treatise" that he "could not disconnect it without making the remainder faulty" [see S. V. Keeling, *Descartes* (London: Oxford University Press, ed. 2, 1968), pp. 17-21]. While Descartes was careful to avoid publishing his strictly "scientific" works in physiology (with the exception of the less controversial *Dioptrics*), he managed to incorporate summaries of his physiological theories in his more "philosophical" works, which included what he hoped would be acceptable theological justifications of his ideas. Thus, the *Discourse on Method*, section V, summarizes portions of the *Treatise of Man*, and the *Principles of Philosophy* (1644) gives in capsule form important elements of his theory of physiological psychology which were later elaborated in *Passions of the Soul* (1649). Many of Descartes' letters [published in the Ernest Adam and Paul Tannery edition, *Oeuvres de Descartes*, (Paris: Leopold Cerf, 1909)] discuss physiological questions, and the letters between Descartes and Plempius [Vol. I, AT] appear in English for the first time in G. A. Lindeboom's *Descartes and Medicine* (Appendix II, 104-122). In addition to the foregoing, Descartes made certain notes at various times, not intended for publication, which were first published posthumously by Foucher de Careil, and which may now be found in Adam and Tannery, 10:207 and 11:545-547. There are also a number of fragments of Descartes' physiological writings which are not published in the Adam and Tannery edition, which T. S. Hall mentions in his list of Descartes' works in *Treatise of Man*, pp. xlv-xlvi. Finally, anyone who reads Descartes' works will note the inseparability of Cartesian science and philosophy, Cartesian medicine and physics, and Cartesian psychology and cosmology, so a thorough investigation of Cartesian physiology would, in its broadest sense, include all of the works of Descartes.

[2] See T. S. Hall's introductory notes to his translation of Descartes' *Treatise of Man* (Cambridge, Massachusetts: Harvard Univ. Press, 1972), p. xxxvii.

[3] Hall, note 2, p. 2.

[4] Translation by T. S. Hall from Descartes' Description of the Human Body (Adam and Tannery vol. XI:223-226). Professor Hall provided the translation of the entire work.

[5] René Descartes, Treatise of Man, trans. T. S. Hall (Cambridge, Massachusetts: Harvard Univ. Press, 1972), p. 1. All subsequent references to this work will be given as Descartes, Treatise.

[6] Descartes, Treatise, pp. 21-22. Fig. 12 is reproduced from engravings in Salomon de Caus, Les raisons des forces mouvantes avec diverses machines tant utilles que plaisantes ausquelles sont adjoints plusieurs desseings de grotes et fontaines (Frankfurt: J. Norton, 1615).

[7] Descartes, Treatise, p. 23. Fig. 13 is Fig. 2 in Hall's edition.

[10] Descartes, Treatise, p. 28.

[11] Descartes, Treatise, p. 30.

[12] Descartes, Treatise, pp. 33-34.

[13] Descartes, Treatise, p. 34. Fig. 15 is Fig. 7 in Hall's edition.

[14] Descartes, Treatise, note 60, p. 34.

[15] Descartes, Treatise, pp. 36-37.

[16] Descartes, Treatise, pp. 37-40.

[17] René Descartes, The World, or Treatise of Light, trans. Michael S. Mahoney (New York: Abaris Books, Inc., 1979), pp. 1-7.

[18] Descartes, Treatise, pp. 68-69.

[19] Descartes, Treatise, pp. 71-72.

[20] Descartes, Treatise, pp. 73-76.

[21] Descartes, Treatise, pp. 72-73.

22 Descartes, Treatise, pp. 77-79. Figs. 16, 17, and 18 are Figs. 23, 24. and 25 repectively in Hall's edition.

23 Descartes, Treatise, pp. 84-85.

24 Descartes, Treatise, note 132, p. 85.

25 Descartes, Treatise, note 132, p. 85.

26 Descartes, Treatise, pp. 86-87.

27 Descartes, Treatise, pp. 87-88.

28 Fig. 20 is Fig. 30 in Hall's edition.

29 Descartes, Treatise, p. 91.

30 Descartes, Treatise, p. 92.

31 Descartes, Treatise, p. 96.

32 Descartes, Treatise, pp. 96-97. Fig. 21 is Fig. 35 in Hall's edition.

33 Descartes, Treatise, p. 100.

34 Descartes, Treatise, pp. 100-101.

35 Descartes, Treatise, pp. 103-104.

36 Descartes, Treatise, note 150, p. 104.

37 Descartes, Treatise, p. 106.

38 Descartes, Treatise, p. 108.

39 Descartes, Treatise, p. 112.

40 René Descartes, The Passions of the Soul, trans. Elizabeth S. Haldane and G. R. T. Ross in The Philosophical Works of Descartes (Cambridge: Cambridge Univ. Press, 1911), Vol. I, p. 340. All subsequent references to this work will be given as Descartes, Passions.

CHAPTER 4:
DESCARTES' USE OF MODELS IN HIS TREATISE OF MAN

Descartes' use of models for scientific explanation has been noted by a number of scholars. E. J. Dijksterhuis, for example, discusses in his The Mechanization of the World Picture the broad aspect of the role of the mechanistic hypothesis in transforming man's image of the world, and seems to be the first to note that Descartes initiated the principle that all of nature was capable of being imitated in a mechanical model.1 Dijksterhuis also notes that Descartes' reason for using such hypothetical models was to guess the true process of natural phenomena, and the mechanisms hidden in them.

The latter is what T. S. Hall refers to as Descartes' role in investigating "the nature of the latent cause, or causes, of the patent phenomena of life."2 Neither Dijksterhuis nor Hall, however, explore the nature of the model that Descartes employed in this investigation.

Another related study by Laurens Laudan, "The Clock Metaphor and Probabilism: The Impact of Descartes on English Methodological Thought, 1650-65," discusses Descartes' employment of the mechanistic metaphor of the clock as a probable hypothesis and its implications for subsequent methodological thought, but does not fully explore Descartes' use of the model.3

On the broader issue of the scientific value of models in reducing all phenomena to a single set of laws, A. C. Crombie writes:

> Descartes brought the equation of natural with artificial and its potential for explanation through models to a systematic conclusion by reducing natural and artificial alike, equally, completely and exclusively to the laws of matter in motion which are the ultimate laws of nature.4

R. C. Lewontin's entry in the *Dictionary of the History of Ideas* characterizes Descartes' work as more than the logical conclusion of the use of models in reducing natural and artificial phenomena to the same set of laws, and proclaims that "modern biology springs from that ur-model [unconditioned response model], the *bête-machine*, described in 1637 by Rene Descartes."5

In an article noting the value of models in the history of psychology, Paul McReynolds states that "the two most important early figures in the renaissance of psychology that began in the seventeenth century were Descartes and Hobbes."6 McReynolds asserts that the clock model of human psychology, employed by both Descartes and Hobbes, was, in comparison to the earlier model of graven images or statues of the ancients, the more influential:

For psychology the influence of clocks as models was both profound and lasting. First, the clock model strongly suggested for psychology, as for all sciences, the themes of regular, recurring, predictable, automatically controlled events, and hence broadened, and hastened the acceptance of the concept of natural law; and second, the amazing precision and complexity of "clockwork" suggested the possibility that living organisms might usefully be conceptualized as machines.[7]

Noting that the computer has replaced the clock as a model in 20th century psychology, McReynolds concludes with a word of caution:

> What can we learn from a survey of the history of psychological models? Several things: first, models are extremely important, perhaps essential, in scientific inquiry; second, models at any given period reflect the current nature and level of science; and, third, there is an ever present danger of taking the model too seriously, of identifying the model with the entity to which it is, in fact, only an analogue.[8]

While Dijksterhuis, Crombie, McReynolds, Lewontin, and others have observed the value of models for the advancement of the biological sciences, and physiological psychology in particular, no researcher has addressed the role of models in Descartes' investigation of the structure and function of the human body. The purpose of this chapter is to investigate 1) the nature of models in general, and 2) the nature of the model used by Descartes in his *Treatise of Man*. Since Descartes' writings in physiology are extensive, this section will be limited to a discussion of the model used in the *Treatise of Man*, with references to his other works as necessary to understand his purpose in using a model.[9]

Definition of Terms

While scientists frequently speak of using models, little has been written on defining various kinds of models, or in exploring the presuppositions and implications of their practice. According to Peirce, a model is an icon, literally embodying the features of interest in the original: "Anything whatever . . . is an icon of anything, in so far as it is like that thing and used as a sign of it."[10]

Arthur Burks follows Peirce in this conception of the model when, in his distinction between a model and a formula, he rather tersely concludes, "A model is an icon, a formula is a symbol."[11] Instancing Bohr's model of the atom as opposed to the more accurate account of the behavior of the atom discovered later, Burks maintains that "it was essential to the success of quantum mechanics to give up the search for models and to be satisfied with more abstract and symbolic formulas."[12]

While the definitions of Peirce and Burks suffice for the familiar construction of miniatures which are isomorphic to the originals that they represent, they are not sufficiently detailed to serve our purposes. Indeed, as McReynolds has observed, there is the danger of taking the model too seriously, of identifying the model with the entity to which it is, in fact, only an analogue. If this iconic aspect of models was their only property, Burks assertion that models had to be abandoned for more sophisticated techniques would be correct.

But Max Black, beginning with the more iconic interpretations of Peirce and Burks, proceeds to explore three other aspects of models.[13] Black acknowledges that these three aspects of models—which, when they predominate constitute "analogue," "mathematical, and "theoretical" models—are part of a continuum of characteristics of models which includes the iconic element.

Since the current discussion does not include Descartes' work on optics, the mathematical aspect of models discussed by Black will not be considered. All other aspects discussed by Black will, however, be treated separately, and then combined to form what will be called a Theoretical Scaled Analogue (TSA), the particular kind of model that Descartes seems to have employed in his major physiological investigations.

Scale Model

Black notes that a scale model is always a model of something, a representation of something for which it stands. This is the particular aspect of models that Peirce calls *iconic*, and holds true in the case of scale models in that they share with their originals a set of features or an identical proportionality of magnitudes, a one-to-one correspondence, subject to rules of interpretation. The primary purpose of scale models is to bring the remote or the unknown to our own level of middle-sized existence.

Analogue Model

An analogue model is designed to reproduce in some *new medium* the structure or pattern of relationships in the original. The analogue model, like the scale model, is a symbolic representation of some real or imaginary original, subject to rules of interpretation for making accurate inferences from the relevant features of the model.

A hydraulic model of electrical current flow is an example of an analogue model, in contrast to a miniature representation of Niagara Falls, which would be called a "scale model". Thus, the analogue model shares with its original not a set of features or an identical proportionality of magnitudes but, more abstractly, the same pattern of relationships. Therefore, the analogue model is iconic in a more abstract way than the scale model, and is dominated by the principle of "isomorphism": the point-by-point correspondence between the relations it embodies and those embodied in the original.

Theoretical Model

A theoretical model, unlike the scale or analogue models, is described but not actually constructed.[14] Black, noting that theoretical models are similar to analogue models in that both create a secondary domain to give insight into the original field of investigation, lists the conditions for the use of theoretical models as a means of defining them:

1. We have an original field of investigation in which *some* facts and regularities have been established (in any form, ranging from disconnected items and crude generalizations to precise laws, possibly organized by a relatively well-articulated theory).

2. A need is felt, either for explaining the given facts and regularities, or for understanding the basic terms applying to the original domain, or for extending the original corpus of knowledge and conjecture, or for connecting it with hitherto disparate bodies of knowledge—in short, a need is felt for further scientific mastery of the original domain.

3. We describe some entities (objects, materials, mechanisms, systems, structures) belonging to a relatively unproblematic, more familiar, or better-organized secondary domain. The postulated properties of these entities are described in whatever detail seems likely to prove profitable.

4. Explicit or implicit rules of correlation are available for translating statements about the secondary field into corresponding statements about the original field.

5. Inferences from the assumptions made in the secondary field are translated by means of the rules of correlation and then independently checked against known or predicted data in the primary domain.[15]

Black notes that the progression from scale to analogue to theoretical models is from the familiar to the "mysterious" (theoretical models) where "mere description of an imaginary but possible structure sufficed to facilitate scientific research."[16] But while certain aspects of models may be seen as a continuum, it is valuable to view each aspect as a discrete property so that relative weights may be assigned to each of these properties in any *particular* model.

Using the foregoing descriptions of scale, analogue, and theoretical models as set forth by Black, and considering Descartes' use of models in his physiological writings, yields what will now be used as a working hypothesis for the remainder of the chapter: that Descartes used a Theoretical Scaled Model (TSA).

Since Black proceeded from the least abstract to the most abstract elements of models—scaled to analogue to theoretical—this will be the order followed in documenting the working hypothesis of this chapter, even though the TSA used by Descartes is—as the name implies—a theoretical model, with scaling and analogy assuming a subordinate role.

Descartes' Use of the Scale Model

It is tempting to see scaled models represented in the illustrations accompanying the text of *Treatise of Man*. The illustrations for the work, however, were added by Louis de La Forge after Descartes' death. Moreover, La Forge explains that, in making his illustrations of the text, he felt "committed less to representing things according to Nature than to rendering intelligible" what Descartes had to say.[17] There is, therefore, no strong iconic element in the original text of the treatise.

There is, however, the element of scaling in the text itself. In writing of the characteristics of the hypothetical Man, Descartes addresses the issue of the reader's knowledge of anatomy:

> If you do not already know them [the parts of the body] sufficiently, you can have them shown to you by some learned anatomist, those at least that are large enough to be seen. As for those which because of their smallness are invisible, I shall be able to make them known to you most simply and clearly by speaking of the movements which depend upon them; so that it remains only for me to explain these movements to you here in proper order and by that means to tell you which of the machine's [latent] functions these [patent] movements represent.[18]

Descartes was in fact using a scaled model for its chief advantage: to bring the remote or the unknown to our own level of middle-sized existence. Or, as T. S. Hall explains, Descartes was "aware of the limitations of sensation," and therefore, "saw himself not as stating the truth but as developing a model—a metaphor—that somehow squared with truth on the one hand and with sensory experience on the other.[19] Hall notes further that this is a process of trying to discover "the nature of the latent cause, or causes, of the patent phenomena of life."[20]

Descartes' Use of the Analogue Model

That Descartes' Man is an analogue of its original, constructed in a new medium, is apparent from the following:

These men will be composed, as we are, of a soul and a body; and I must first separately describe for you the body; then, also separately, the soul; and finally I must show you how these two natures would have to be joined and united to constitute men resembling us. I assume their body to be but a statue, an earthen machine formed intentionally by God to be as much as possible like us. Thus not only does He give it externally the shapes and colors of all the parts of our bodies; He also places inside it all the pieces required to make it walk, eat, breathe, and imitate whichever of our own functions can be imagined to proceed from mere matter and to depend entirely on the arrangement of our organs.

We see clocks, artificial fountains, mills, and similar machines which, though made entirely by man, lack not the power to move, of themselves, in various ways. And I think you will agree that the present machine could have even more sorts of movements than I have imagined and more ingenuity than I have assigned, for our supposition is that it was created by God.[21]

Descartes proceeds to construct his model so that there is a one-to-one correspondence between its functions and those of its original (to the extent of his knowledge of the functions of the original).

Descartes' God is described as a master craftsman, differing from man only in His ability to construct more cleverly designed machines.

Again, as with the illustrations, La Forge's commentary is misleading, since he purports to show how the Cartesian models of function can really be made to work.[22]

Descartes' Use of the Theoretical Model

Descartes' Man is a theoretical model in that it is described but not constructed. As with the analogue aspect of the model, the theoretical aspect invents a secondary domain to give insight into the original field of investigation: the mechanical hypothesis, proceeding from Descartes' Universal Mathematics, set forth in Rule IV in his *Rules for Direction of the Mind*.

To further explore the theoretical aspect of Descartes' model of man, it is necessary to consider other of his writings in respect to Black's five previously mentioned conditions for the use of theoretical models, each of which will now be addressed in turn as they apply to the work of Descartes.

We have an original field of investigation in which some facts and regularities have been established (in any form, ranging from disconnected items and crude generalizations to precise laws, possibly organized by a relatively well-articulated theory).

In *Rules for the Direction of the Mind*, Descartes defines Science as "true and evident cognition."[24] He then notes that "there are two ways by which we arrive at the knowledge of facts, viz. by experience and by deduction."[25] Since "none of the mistakes which men make . . . are due to faulty inferences," Descartes writes, "they are caused merely by the fact that we found upon a basis of poorly comprehended experiences, or that propositions are posited which are hasty and groundless."

It is for this reason that Descartes asserts "the great superiority in certitude of Arithmetic and Geometry to other sciences," since "the former alone deal with an object so pure and uncomplicated, that they need make no assumptions at all which experience renders uncertain, but wholly consist in the rational deduction of consequences."[27] The "object" of Mathematics and Geometry, Descartes tells us, is "order and measurement.[28]

Thus, the original field of investigation which is organized by a relatively well-articulated theory is mathematics, but a particular kind of mathematics:

> But as I considered the matter carefully it gradually came to light that all those matters only were referred to Mathematics in which order and measurement are investigated, and that it makes no difference whether it be in numbers, figures, stars, sounds or any other object that the question of measurement arises. This, I perceived, was called 'Universal Mathematics', not a far fetched designation, but one of long standing which has passed into current use, because in this science is contained everything on account of which the others are called parts of Mathematics.[29]

The Universal Mathematics holds certain problems in common with its subordinate sciences, but is free from many of the difficulties existing in these sciences since the latter have a "special subject matter."

The first seven of the *Rules for Direction of the Mind*, if they were to stand alone, would support the role that the traditional interpretation of the history of modern philosophy has assigned to the Cartesian Method: a strict mathematical rationalism which is held to be adamant in its resistance to experience as a source of scientific truth. However, with Rule VIII, Descartes recognizes that the realm of the Universal Mathematics—the mind or understanding—may be insufficiently equipped to handle the objects of "Physics" (the physical sciences), so that the seeker of truth is "here forced to pause at the threshold."[31]

> A need is felt, either for explaining the given facts and regularities, or for understanding the basic terms applying to the original domain, or for extending the original corpus of knowledge and conjecture, or for connecting it with hitherto disparate bodies of knowledge—in short, a need is felt for further scientific mastery of the original domain.

Descartes acknowledges that "while it is the understanding alone which is capable of knowing, it yet is either helped or hindered by three other faculties, namely, imagination, sense, and memory."[32] As a matter of definition, Descartes states that:

> It is one and the same agency which, when applying itself along with the imagination to the common sense, is said to see, touch, etc.; if applying itself to the imagination alone in so far as that is endowed with diverse impressions, it is said to remember; if it turn to the imagination in order to create fresh impressions, it is said to imagine or conceive; finally if it act alone it is said to understand.[33]

So the same faculty "in correspondence with those various functions is called either pure understanding, or imagination, or memory, or sense."[34]

Descartes, with Rule VIII, has reached the point where the understanding—in itself the only faculty capable of the "true and evident cognition" which is Science—must be assisted by the corporeal faculties. The general problem of the Cartesian Method, then, is that of determining whether there are objects for the knowledge of which the pure understanding is not sufficient.[35]

The original domain of the Universal Mathematics—the understanding or intellect—must, then, be extended into the corporeal domain (see Figure 22 for this author's understanding of the general relationship of Descartes' "faculties").

> We describe some entities (objects, materials, mechanisms, systems, structures) belonging to a relatively unproblematic, more familiar, or better-organized secondary domain. The postulated properties of these entities are described in whatever detail seems likely to prove profitable.

The secondary domain, then, becomes the world of the physical, the objects of physical science. Descartes' Method provides a role for experience in that it places the understanding in direct contact with the objects of physical science, as a necessary aid to the understanding:

> Consequently, whatever our Understanding may believe as to the truth of the matter, those abstract entities are never given to our imagination as separate from the objects in which they adhere.[37]

Now, the properties of the objects given to the imagination involve the concept of extension:

> By extension we understand whatever has length, breadth, and depth, not inquiring
> whether it be a real body or merely space; nor does it appear to require further
> explanation, since there is nothing more easily perceived by our imagination.[38]

As various aspects of extension, Descartes includes dimension, unity, and figure, all of which are means of using the notion of extension to define the concepts of weight, speed, quantity, and shape of an object or objects.[39]

The process of investigating phenomena in the physical world involves a procedure in which the mixed phenomena presented to the senses are "split up" into "the various sections beyond which analysis cannot go in minuteness."[40]

While the foregoing seems to be only a process of reducing phenomena into mathematically describable units for the purpose of dealing with abstract qualities, this is not the case:

> I have no hesitation in saying that it was not the case that this part of our method
> was invented for the purpose of dealing with mathematical problems, but rather that
> mathematics should be studied almost solely for the purpose of training us in this
> method.[41]

The distinction between mathematics and physics becomes apparent in the following:

> Yet all these subdivisions are exactly similar if considered merely from the point of
> view of dimension, as we ought to regard them both here and in the science of
> Mathematics. It falls rather to Physics to inquire whether they are founded on anything
> real.[42]

The question of the *reality* of the subject matter under consideration, then, falls to a method similar to that used in mathematics, but with recourse to what Descartes calls the "simple natures" into which phenomena can be subdivided. Descartes' appeal to the secondary domain of sensory experience becomes, then, an integral part of his Method.

> Explicit or implicit rules of correlation are available for translating statements about
> the secondary field into corresponding statements about the original field.

The question of how the secondary field of the physical is to be related by the corporeal faculties to the original field of the Universal Mathematics in the pure Understanding demands certain rules of correlation.

Since there are certain "knowns" in the realm of the pure intellect, the process of extending knowledge into the realm of the unknown becomes one of finding the degree of correspondence between certain interrelationships among the "simple natures" of the unknown and similar interrelationships in the known (what Descartes calls the "common nature"):

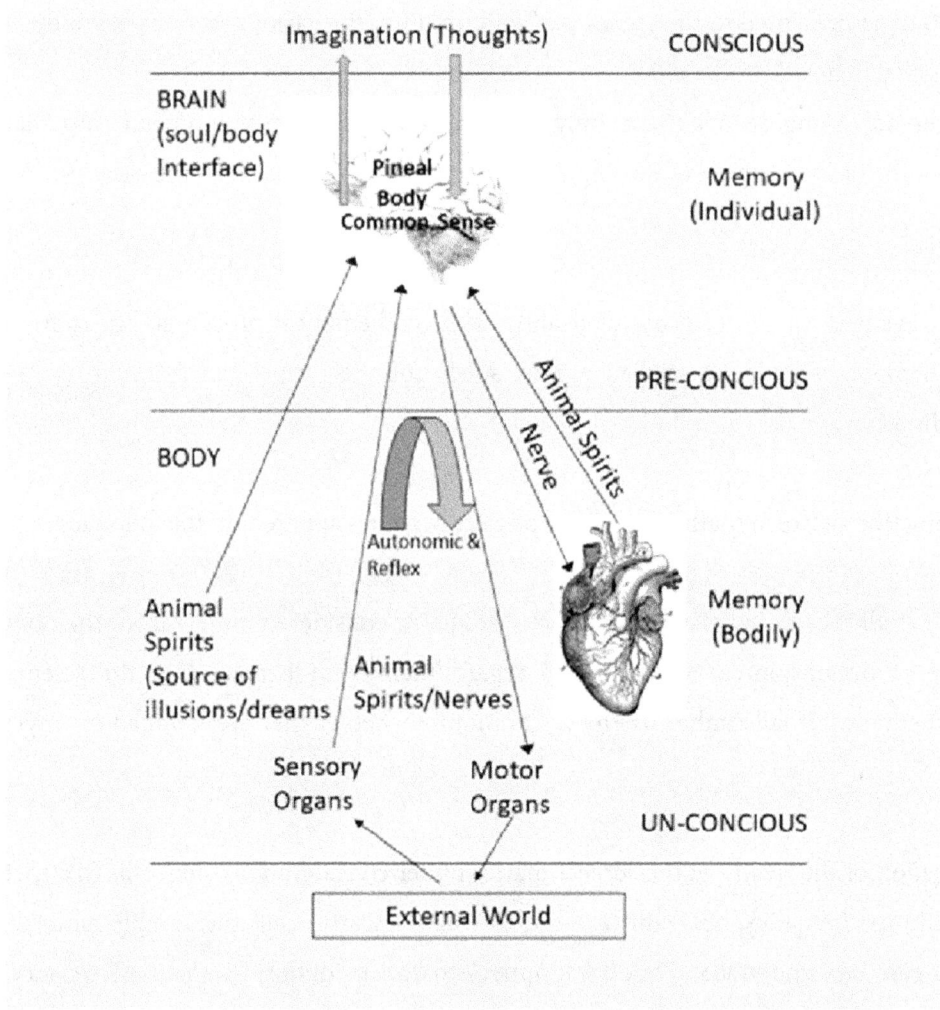

Figure 22.

Schematic of Descartes' notion of "faculties"

(the relationship of the soul to various bodily functions).

But we shall believe ourselves to have attained whatever in this matter can be achieved by our human faculties, if we discern with all possible distinctness that mixture of entities or natures already known which produces just those effects which we notice…Note that the only reason why preparation is required for comparison that is not of this nature is the fact that the common nature we spoke of does not exist equally in both, but is complicated with certain other relations or ratios. The chief part of our human industry consists merely in so transmuting these ratios as to show clearly a uniformity between the matter sought for and something else already known.

Next we must mark that nothing can be reduced to this uniformity, save that which admits of a greater and a less, and that all such matter is included under the term magnitude.[43]

Descartes' assertion that the realm of the physical and the realm of the universal share certain ratios or interrelationships is the basis of the "mechanistic hypothesis" which he develops in the later treatises, *The World*, and *Treatise of Man*.

The rule for establishing a correlation between statements about the secondary field and statements about the original field is, then, to reduce the secondary field into "simple natures" which are capable of being expressed as magnitudes, the latter of which involves certain ratios or interrelationships common to the original field. The method in which this is achieved is discussed in the next section.

Inferences from the assumptions made in the secondary field are translated by means of the rules of correlation and then independently checked against known or predicted data in the primary domain.

The *Rules*, which Descartes developed in theory, were only later put to the test in the physical sciences. Following the completion of the *Rules* in 1628, Descartes turned to the writing of his *Treatise of Light*, the component parts of which were *The World* and *Treatise of Man*. In a letter to Mersenne, dated April 5, 1632, Descartes reported progress on the work, and said that it contained "a general description of the stars, the heavens, and the earth, as well as bodies on the earth." Concerning the latter, he expressed his desire to "show the way to an understanding of them through the combined use of experiment and reason."[45]

A few months later, Descartes wrote again to Mersenne:

In my *World* I shall speak somewhat more of man than I had thought to before, because I shall try to explain all his principal functions. I have already written about those that pertain to life, such as the digestion of food, the beating of the pulse, the distribution of nutrients, etc., and the five senses. Now I am dissecting the heads of different animals in order to explain what imagination, memory, etc. consist of.[46]

That his *Rules* were difficult to apply to the physical sciences is evident in sections of the *Discourse on Method* (1632), which was written following the completion of *The World* and *Treatise of Man*:

I remarked also respecting experiments, that they become so much more necessary the more one is advanced in knowledge, for to begin with it is better to make use simply of those which present themselves spontaneously to our senses, and of which we could not be ignorant provided that we reflected ever so little, rather than to seek out those which are more rare and recondite; the reason of this is that those which are more rare often mislead us so long as we do not know the causes of the more common, and the fact that the circumstances on which they depend are almost always so particular and so minute that it is very difficult to observe them.[47]

After proceeding to recount the Method he has developed earlier, he notes that it is effective in general:

But I must also confess that the power of nature is so ample and so vast, and these principles are so simple and general, that I observed hardly any particular effect as to which I could not at once recognize that it might be deduced from the principles in many different ways; and my greatest difficulty is usually to discover in which of these ways the effect does depend upon them. As to that, I do not know any other plan but again to try to find experiments of such a nature that their result is not the same if it has to be explained by the other.[48]

Two points should be noted in the foregoing: the problem of many phenomena being beyond the ability of man's limited sensory perception, and the need to develop some experimental means of separating true from false hypotheses which from all appearances are equiprobable. These problems were not to be fully addressed by Descartes until the publication of his *Principles of Philosophy* (1644).

The first problem relates to the concept of scaling in models. Having made the assertion (in the *Rules*) that "simple natures" expressed in terms of magnitudes represent the essence of material things, Descartes can extrapolate from the world of the visible to the world of the invisible:

But since I assign determinate figures, magnitudes and motions to the insensible particles of bodies, as if I had seen them, whereas I admit that they do not fall under the senses, someone will perhaps demand how I have come to my knowledge of them. To this I reply that I first considered generally the most simple and best understood principles implanted in our understanding by nature, and examined the principal differences that could be found between the magnitudes, figures and situations of bodies insensible on account of their smallness alone, and what sensible effects could be produced by the various ways in which they impinge on one another. And finally, when I found like effects in the bodies perceived by our senses, I considered that they might have been produced from a similar concourse of such bodies, especially as no other mode of explaining them could be suggested. And for this end the example of certain bodies made by art was of service to me, for I can see no difference between these and natural bodies, excepting that the effects of machines depend for the most part on the operation of certain instruments, which, since men necessarily make them, must always be large enough to be capable of being easily perceived by the senses. The effects of natural causes, on the other hand, almost always depend on certain organs minute enough to escape every sense. And it is certain that there are no rules in mechanics which do not hold good in physics, of which mechanics forms a part or species [so that all that is artificial is also natural]; for it is not less natural for a clock, made of the requisite number of wheels, to indicate the hours, than for a tree which has sprung from this or that seed, to produce a particular fruit. Accordingly, just as those who apply themselves to the consideration of automata, when they know the use of a certain machine and see some of its parts, easily infer from these the manner in which others which they have not seen are made, so from considering the sensible effects and parts of natural bodies, I have endeavoured to discover the nature of the imperceptible causes and insensible parts contained in them.[49]

T. S. Hall refers to the foregoing passage as Descartes' "Micro-mechanics," the extension of his mechanistic hypothesis to the study of physiology. Descartes has, in fact, proceeded from the realm of the "pure" Understanding to the realm of the visible corporeal, and thence to the realm of the invisible corporeal, by the methodical development and application of certain rules of correlation involving the concept of magnitudes and the assumption that their interrelationships are preserved throughout these various domains.

The second problem, the need for experiments to test hypotheses, is addressed by Descartes as follows:

But here it may be said that although I have shown how all natural things can be formed, we have no right to conclude on this account that they were produced by these causes. For just as there may be two clocks made by the same workman, which though they indicate the time equally well and are externally in all respects similar, yet in nowise resemble one another in the composition of their wheels, so doubtless there is an infinity of different ways in which all things that we see could be formed by the great Artificer [without it being possible for the mind of man to be aware of which of these means he has chosen to employ]. This I most freely admit; and I believe that I have done all that is required of me if the causes I have assigned are such that they correspond to all the phenomena manifested by nature [without inquiring whether it is by their means or by others that they are produced]. And it will be sufficient for the usages of life to know such causes, for medicine and mechanics and in general all these arts to which the knowledge of physics subserves, have for their end only those effects which are sensible, and which are accordingly to be reckoned among the phenomena of nature.

So, in the realm of physical sciences, the interrelationship of certain "simple natures," if they can be duplicated in models to reproduce natural phenomena, are to be taken as the closest thing to "true and evident cognition"—Science—that the mind can achieve.

It is evident that Descartes struggled with the question of "true and evident cognition," beginning with the establishment of a method upon which the ontological foundations of the *Universal Mathematics* could be based (*Rules* and *Discourse*), and then with the development of models designed to extend knowledge into the realm of the physical (*Treatise of Man* and *The World*), both macro- and micro-scopic, and ending with the concession that the ontological basis of "physics" may be beyond the reach of the human mind.

Noting this progression in Descartes' writings, Phillip R. Sloan maintains that the radical Cartesian dualism was a response to the reawakening of Pyrrhonian scepticism in the Renaissance."[51] This form of scepticism, if it had been allowed to prevail, would have argued for a state of intellectual suspense that would have undercut any claims to scientific certainty. Realizing this, Sloan maintains, Descartes set out to refute the Phrrhonist philosophy and establish a firm ontological basis for his scientific work:

The emergence of the Cartesian physiological synthesis can be followed as we observe the apparent ordering of stages of Descartes confrontation with the pyrrhonist problem. As Descartes repeatedly emphasizes, the eventual separation of mind from body depends on a precise sequence of argumentation which must be followed if the desired conclusion is to follow. As we can discern in each of the foundation texts of the Cartesian metaphysics—the *Discourse, Medications, Principles of Philosophy*, and the possible early *Récherche de la vérité*, the following steps in the argument can be discerned....⁵

The steps discussed by Sloan are:

1. Initially, there is some statement of the uncertainty of knowledge, following the arguments of the sceptics against the senses. The intent of the statement is to show the uncertainty of knowledge, particularly knowledge which is presumed to have its source in sensory testimony.
2. The second stage of the argument is to push the sceptical doubts beyond their utilization by the sceptics to create a state of intellectual suspense to the point that extra-mental existence is a possible delusion of the senses.
3. The third and final stage of the argument is that the world of sense, destroyed by a radicalized Pyrrhonic doubt, can only be approached indirectly, depending always on the ontological proofs of a non-deceiving God who guarantees the conformity
4. of clear and distinct ideas to events in the material realm.⁵³

From this ordered argument, Sloan states that two main consequences emerge:

1. The divine guarantee of certainty in knowledge of the material world holds *only* if events and processes in the material world are understood in their "mathematical" dimensions. In other words, the understanding of all natural events and processes is possible only in terms of an "analysis" into the primary motions and qualities of an extensionally-conceived matter, and the primary laws which govern matter and motion in the material world.
2. The relation of the immaterial soul or mind with the body is necessarily indirect and involves no relationship of vitalization.⁵⁴

The implication of the second consequence noted by Sloan is extremely important in the consideration of Descartes' use of models in that the metaphor of the machine was no longer simply an analogy, but a literal parallel of processes occurring within the human body.

The importance of this radical mechanism and its implications for the use of models in the biological sciences noted earlier in the chapter in a quotation from A. C. Crombie bears repeating:

Descartes brought the equation of natural with artificial and its potential for explanation through models to a systematic conclusion by reducing natural and artificial alike, equally, completely and exclusively to the laws of matter in motion which were the ultimate laws of nature.[55]

The importance of Descartes' model of man in the history of physiology in general, and physiological psychology in particular, will be discussed in the next chapter.

Notes to Chapter 4

[1] E. J. Dijksterhuis, The Mechanization of the World Picture, trans. C. Dikshoorn (Oxford: Clarendon Press, 1961), p. 415.

[2] I. S. Hall, "Descartes' Physiological Method: Position, Principles, Examples," Journal of the History of Biology, 3, No. 1 (1970), 55.

[3] Laurens Laudan, "The Clock Metaphor and Probabilism: The Impact of Descartes on English Methodological Thought, 1650-65," Annals of Science, 22, No. 2 (1966), 73-104.

[4] A. C. Crombie, "Marin Mersenne (1588-1648) and the Seventeenth-Century Problem of Scientific Acceptability," Physis, 17, Nos. 3-4 (1970), 19.

[5] R. C. Lewontin, "Biological Models," in the Dictionary of the History of Ideas (New York: Charles Scribner's Sons, 1973), p. 242.

[6] Paul McReynolds, "Statues, Clocks, and Computers: The History of Models in Psychology," Proceedings of the 79th Annual Convention of the American Psychological Association (1971), Vol. 6, 716.

[7] McReynolds, p. 716.

[8] McReynolds, p. 716.

[9] For a listing of Descartes' physiological writings, see note 1, Chapter III of this work.

[10] Charles S. Peirce, Collected Papers of Charles Saunders Peirce (Cambridge: Harvard Univ. Press, 1931-1935), II, ed. Charles Hartshorne and Paul Weiss, p. 247.

[11] Arthur W. Burks, Chance, Cause, Reason: An Inquiry into the Nature of Scientific Evidence (Chicago: Univ. of Chicago Press, 1963), p. 32.

[12] Burks, p. 32.

[13] Max Black, Models and Metaphors (New York: Cornell Univ. Press, 1962), pp. 219-243.

[14] It should be noted that Burks, unlike Black, distinguishes between models and theories: "The words 'model' and 'theory' are used in various ways, often interchangeably, but for our purposes we distinguish them sharply. A hypothetical, constructed, imagined, or actual structure or system is a model of an actual system or aspect of reality when it is sufficiently similar to or isomorphic with that system or aspect of reality. A theory is a statement or system of statements asserting something about the universe, a part of it, or some aspect of it. Some theories are statements about models, saying, in effect, that the given model is similar to reality in certain respects." (p. 31).

[15] While Black's ideas on scale and analogue models were summarized, his description of theoretical models is listed verbatim (p. 230) since this model (or rather, this aspect of models) will be strongest in Descartes' writings.

[16] Black, p. 239.

[17] La Forge's remarks are on p. 326 of the first French edition of Descartes' Treatise of Man (Paris: Charles Angot, 1664).

[18] René Descartes, Treatise of Man, trans. T. S. Hall (Cambridge: Harvard Univ. Press, 1972), pp. 4-5. Subsequent references to the Treatise of Man will be to this edition.

[19] Hall, "Descartes' Physiological Method," p. 74.

[20] Hall, p. 74.

[21] Descartes, Treatise, pp. 1-4.

[22] See T. S. Hall's Introduction to his translation of Treatise of Man, p. xli.

[23] This interpretation is shared by Peter Pav, currently at Eckerd College, who notes in personal correspondence with this author that 'though Descartes was an avid physiologist, both thinking and doing things physiological his whole life, his main thrust was not principally to further physiology itself, but to shore up and advertise his new approach to the mechanistic philosophy.

Replacing non mechanistic concepts like faculties by pushes and pulls was a big part of that program." (Undated correspondence received 12 March 81).

[24] René Descartes, Rules for the Direction of the Mind, trans. Elizabeth S. Haldane and G. R. T. Ross, in The Philosophical Works of Descartes (Cambridge: Cambridge Univ. Press, 1911), Vol. I, p. 3. All subsequent references to the Rules and the Meditations will be to this translation and volume.

[25] Rules, p. 4. See also Gerd Buchdahl, "Descartes' Anticipation of a 'Logic of Scientific Discovery,'" in Scientific Change: Historical Studies in the Intellectual, Social and Technical Conditions for Scientific Discovery and Technical Invention, from Antiquity to the Present, ed. A. C. Crombie (London: Heinemann, 1962), pp. 399-417 for discussion of Descartes' particular kind of deduction.

[26] Rules, p. 5.

[27] Rules, p. 5.

[28] Rules, p. 13.

[29] Rules, p. 13.

[30] Rules, p. 13.

[31] Rules, p. 23.

[32] Rules, p. 27.

[33] Rules, p. 39.

[34] Rules, p. 39.

[35] For the role of experience in the Cartesian Method, see Alan Gewirtz, "Experience and the Non-Mathematical in the Cartesian Method," Journal of the History of Ideas, 2, No. (194), 183-210; and Ralph M. Blake, et al., "The Role of Experience in Descartes' Theory of Method," in Theories of Scientific Method: The Renaissance through the Nineteenth Century, ed. Edward H. Madden (Seattle: University of Washington Press, 1960), pp. 75-103.

36 Constructed from Descartes' Rules, Discourse, Treatise of Man, and Passions of the Soul. Note the interaction between the objects of sensory perception and the intellect through the "imagination." Also note that there is always the possibility of divine inspiration (dotted line from "God").

37 Rules, p. 58.

38 Rules, p. 57.

39 Rules, pp. 61-65.

40 Rules, pp. 49, 54. Rule XIII for the mathematical sciences is extended to the physical sciences in Rule XIV.

41 Rules, p. 57.

42 Rules, p. 62.

43 Rules, pp. 55-56.

44 In both works Descartes assumes three elements differing in the size and shape of their constituent particles.

45 René Descartes, Oeuvres de Descartes, ed. Charles Adam and Paul Tannery (Paris, 1897-1913), I, p. 243. Translation by author.

46 Adam and Tannery, I, p. 263. Regarding Descartes' work on the brain, Edwin Clarke and Kenneth Dewhurst, An Illustrated History of Brain Function (Berkeley: Univ. of California Press, 1972), p. 68 note in their commentary on Descartes' illustration of the brain that his depiction of the cerebral and cerebellar convolutions is the most accurate encountered until after his time, far exceeding the accuracy of Vesalius in this area.

47 René Descartes, Discourse on the Method, in Haldane and Ross, I, pp. 299-300.

48 Discourse, p. 121.

49 René Descartes, Principles of Philosophy, in Haldane and Ross, I, pp. 299-300.

[50] *Principles*, p. 300.

[51] Phillip R. Sloan, "Descartes, the Sceptics, and the Rejection of Vitalism in Seventeenth-Century Physiology," *Studies in the History and Philosophy of Science*, 8, No. 1 (1977), 1-28.

[52] Sloan, p. 15.

[53] The steps are a summary of Sloan, pp. 15-16.

[54] The consequences are a summary of Sloan, pp. 16-17.

[55] Crombie, note 4 this chapter.

CHAPTER 5:
THE CARTESIAN INFLUENCE

T. S. Hall notes:

> The influence of Descartes was felt at first on the broad conceptual level—through the urgent application of his materialistic and mechanistic ideas—and only later, and through the work of others, on the level of concrete detail.[1]

What Hall refers to as Descartes' influence "on the broad concept level" is further developed by Phillip R. Sloan who states:

> At the heart of the Scientific Revolution was a basic struggle not simply over fact, but more importantly over the foundational questions as to what constitutes experience, how mind and language connect with the world, and the grounds and sources of natural knowledge.[2]

Sloan notes that two major philosophical influences, Aristotelian and Platonic, vied for dominance in the 17th century:

> Physical theory of the early seventeenth-century had, on the one hand, made almost axiomatic the conclusion that the testimony of the senses and the evidence supplied by ordinary experience meeting the Aristotelian criteria concerning proper medium and conditions, was inherently deceptive. The Copernican theory had involved, as Galileo was to put it, a great 'ravishment' of the senses, which could not be accorded with an Aristotelian theory of experience. Galilean mechanics had made a further supplantation of Aristotelian Realism as the basis of physical science, replacing it with a quasi-Platonic intuition of ideal mathematical form behind appearance which could correct the testimony of sense in accord with the demands of mathematical formalism.[3]

Sloan maintains that these competing philosophies played into the hands of the sceptics of the time:

This epistemological incoherence between two very prominent wings of the developing new science was but one factor which a pyrrhonist could utilize to create a suspense of judgment with regards to the new science in the late Renaissance. The internecine struggles within the new science itself, reflected in such phenomena as the antimony wars among the Paracelsians, the disputes between the circularists and Keplerians in astronomy, and the general conflict between the esoteric and exoteric approaches to the new science all provided potential ammunition for a rejection of the claims of the new science on Pyrrhonist grounds.[4]

It was against this background that Descartes' philosophy developed and was to have a broad conceptual influence.

As noted toward the end of the last chapter, Descartes responded to the skeptical attacks on the certainty of knowledge in the sciences. The Cartesian answer to what was in many respects the critical question confronting the new science meant to accept a mechanical philosophy with its "clearly and distinctly conceivable ideas" which, fortunately for Descartes, included the belief in the circulation of the blood.

But, as Sloan notes, Descartes' influence was strongest at the conceptual, not the empirical, level:

The firmness with which Descartes' physiology apparently took hold in the mid-seventeenth-century would seem to indicate that something more important than empirical considerations were at stake. By 1659, over half of the medical faculty at Leyden were self-professed Cartesians. And in spite of the numerous divergences that can readily be detected on specific physiological issues between Descartes and the multitude of mechanical physiologists of the latter part of the century, Descartes' primacy in establishing this research programme would seem well evidenced from the statement by the Danish anatomist Niels Stensen in 1666:

Descartes... was the first who dared to explain all the functions of man, and especially of the brain, in a mechanical manner. Other authors describe man; Descartes puts before us merely a machine, but by means of this he very clearly exposed the ignorance of others who have treated of man, and opened up for us a way by which to investigate the use of the other parts of the body as no one has done before.[5]

Sloan also finds two examples of Descartes' influence on the conceptual level in the scientific research described in the treatises of the two earliest proponents of a thoroughgoing mechanical physiology: Cornelius van Hoogehlande (1590-1651), a physician of Leyden and a personal friend of Descartes, and the more historically important physician, Henry Le Roy (Regius) (1598-1679), professor of Medicine and Botany at the University of Utrecht from 1638-1679.[6] In 1646, both men published works which they claimed set forth new applications of mechanical explanations to the "animal oeconomy" (the name for physiology at the time).

The most important aspect of Hoogehlande's work, at least from the standpoint of demonstrating a Cartesian influence, was his attack on the adherents to "occult causes" in the explanation of the motion of the heart and blood. In reply to these occultists, Hoogehlande insisted upon explanations which are clearly and distinctly conceived:

> First…all natural activities, motions, effects and alterations of natural bodies are produced by or depend on the definite figures and motions of bodies.
>
> Secondly…no explanation or demonstration can be true or indubitable which is not mechanical.
>
> Thirdly…all philosophers now seeking the underlying causes of things implicitly admit that explanations by occult (antipathies, sympathies, attractions) or manifest (cold, heat, etc.) qualities cannot be accepted for the true or genuine explanations, but desire other more solid and intelligible kinds, namely mechanical ones.
>
> And Forthly, if obscure premisses or occult terms or qualities are summoned to explain the operations of nature, then certainly what is explained will be even more obscure ….[7]

What Hoogehlande was clearly calling for the banishment of psychistic explanations of life phenomena.

In the conclusion of his work, Hoogehlande makes explicit his indebtedness to Descartes for his belief in mechanical explanations of biological functions:

> But indeed, that incomparable man, René Descartes, has generously blessed the age in which we live with the splendor of his intellect…, so that whoever follows in his footsteps can, without difficulty, distinguish doubt from certainty and truth from falsity…. Furthermore, it is the good fortune of future ages that now whatever is intelligible in material things, namely, quantity, figure…, and local motion can, at least in general, be immediately distinguished from what is obscure.[8]

What Hoogehlande sees in Cartesianism is a demand and a rationale for a certain *kind* of analysis, a reductive mechanical one, rather than empirical results.

Regius represents an important figure in the initial exposition of the mechanistic conception of physiology for two reasons. First, Regius had excellent medical credentials, having received his M.D. from Padua as a student of Santorio Sanctorius, and was the first Cartesian physician to occupy a teaching post on the medical faculty of the newly-established University of Utrecht in 1638.[9] Second, Regius' reworking and extension of the Cartesian physiology was known to foreign physicians at an early date and served as a probable route by which mechanical physiology gained its very early penetration into professional circles.[10]

In his work, Regius endorses the Cartesian analogy of the animal with a clock or automaton whose functions are to be seen solely as a product of the arrangement and dispositions of its parts.[11] Regius goes on at length in giving a purely mechanical analysis of the innate heat, denying traditional vitalistic explanations in favor of the Cartesian "fire without light" produced by fermentation. Detailed mechanical accounts, some comparing and some differing from Descartes', are also given for respiration, nutrition, excretion, and generation.

Regius defended his mechanistic explanations of life phenomena against critics by arguing that explanations of natural processes in terms of primary properties of matter, motions and mechanical actions were to be adopted because only these offered certainty and intelligibility. He argued, for example, that explanations in terms of invisible particles were favorable to accepting vitalistic "principles" and "first causes":

> [Substances] are divided into either insensible or sensible parts. The insensible parts are those which, by reason of their minuteness, escape the senses, and are perceived in all natural things only by reason. Examples of such include the branched particles comprising oil; and the oblong and flexible particles constituting water....
>
> These [insensible parts] are plainly inferred from the subtlety, solidity, sharpness, resistance, fluidity, oiliness, aqueosity, salinity, and all the innumerable other qualities of bodies subsequently being explained. For by putting forward these insensible particles, the explanation of the qualities of bodies is clear and distinct, whereas by the denial of them, it is obscure or confused.[12]

That Regius defended explanations of life phenomena by positing invisible, yet material, forces indicates that he was influenced by what T. S. Hall finds was the most important Cartesian doctrine, "that the goal of physiological inquiry is to discover the latent equivalents of patent biological function."[13] As Hall notes, Descartes "was notoriously aware of the limitations of reason."[14] With such an awareness, Descartes posited that the laws of mechanics applied below the level of visibility as they did at the level of visibility. This assertion had enormous consequences for the study of physiology, even though it could not be proven in Descartes' time, primarily because models of hypothetical mechanisms could be developed and tested at a visible level. Hall points out that Descartes was aware of this approach to research by quoting a passage from the *Principles* expressing the wish that:

> …what I shall write be taken as only an hypothesis which may be very far from the truth, [but] even though it be such, I shall think I have done much if all the things which shall be deduced from it are entirely conformant to experience; because if that be the case, it will be no less useful to life than if it were true, because one will be able to use it just as well in arranging natural causes to produce desired effects.[15]

While Descartes' mechanical explanations of life phenomena were influential on continental Europe, Harvey's work in England pointed in the opposite direction. Early in his career Harvey simply ignored mechanism, but later he resisted it deliberately. As Theodore M. Brown points out, Harvey's negative attitude influenced research undertaken in the 1650s by Francis Glisson at the London College of Physicians and by Robert Boyle at Oxford.[16]

Probably the greatest Cartesian influence in England came about indirectly when, a few months after the 1637 publication of Descartes' *Discourse on the Method*, Kenelm Digby, a friend of both Hobbes and Descartes, acquired copies and passed them on to Hobbes in England with the following letter, dated October 4, 1637:

> Sir
>
> I come now with this to make good what I promised you in my last: which is to putt Monsieur des Cartes (whom Mydorge so much admireth) his book into your hands. I doubt not but you will say this is a production of a most vigorous and strong braine: and that if he were as accurate in his metaphysicall part as he is in his experience, he had carryed the palme from all men living: which nevertheless he peradventure hath done. I shall be very glad to heare your opinion of him: and so in hast I take my leave and rest,
>
> Your true friend and servant
> Kenelm Digby[17]

In the same year that Hobbes received Descartes' work, he planned to write a three part *Elements of Philosophy* : part one, *de corpore*, on physics or matter in motion; part two, *de homine*, on human psychology based upon the physics; and part three, *de cive*, on government or the state based upon human psychology.[18]

With the increasing civil disruptions in England in 1640, Hobbes left for France and remained there eleven years. During the course of his stay in France, Hobbes associated with other English royalist exiles and with members of the Mersenne circle. Hobbes also kept up with his philosophical and scientific studies and writings, writing and publishing *de cive* in 1642, and *Leviathan*, an expanded English version of *de cive*, which he did not publish until 1651.[19]

The Introduction of *Leviathan* bears obvious similarity to Descartes' earlier description of man in his *Discourse on the Method*, where the concept of man as an automaton was developed:

> Nature, the art whereby God hath made and governs the world, is by the *art* of man, as in many other things, so in this also imitated, that it can make an artificial animal. For seeing life is but a motion of limbs, the beginning whereof is in some principal part within; why may we not say, that all *automata* (engines that move themselves by springs and wheels as doth a watch) have an artificial life? For what is the *heart*, but a *spring*; and the *nerves*, but so many *strings*; and the joints, but so many *wheels*, giving motion to the whole body, such as was intended by the artificer?[20]

Aside from Hobbes' attraction to Descartes' notion of the machine analogy for man's body was his elaboration of Descartes' ideas regarding sense experience, memory, fancy, and judgment in the act of cognition. All experience, Hobbes maintained, was some special form of motion. Sensation, for example, was a continuation of that motion which had impinged upon the sense organs, transmitting its motion through the nerves to the brain. Descartes had taught that in higher mental functions the soul, by means of the pineal gland, controlled the passage of an impulse from a nerve to the appropriate channels in the brain; but Hobbes did not require the intervention of the soul, for motion in the brain was sufficient. Since there was no need for the soul, will was simply the last appetite, or the last fear, which in the course of deliberation precipitated overt movement.[21]

Hobbes had succeeded in carrying Descartes' mechanical account of brain function one step further to offer a mechanistic explanation not only for sense and motion, but also the ultimate "human" faculty—reason. The implications for philosophy and religion were enormous, and Hobbes did not hesitate to venture so far as to offer a mechanical account of the process of the poetic and literary imagination. In Hobbes' answer to Davenant's Preface to *Gondibert*, there is a mechanistic alternative proposed for the act of artistic creation in contrast to earlier practices of attributing such acts to forces outside the mind of man, including the ancient Muses.[22]

Aside from the tremendous implications for British philosophy and aesthetic theory, Hobbes' mechanistic account of mental phenomena included a theory regarding the *order* of mental events that was to greatly influence the history of psychology in England. Essentially, Hobbes asserted that the order of events occurring within the brain depends upon the sequence of the original experiences caused by stimulation coming from the outside world:

> And those motions that immediately succeeded one another in the sense, continue also together after Sense: in so much as the former comming again to take place, and be praedominant, the latter followeth, by coherence of the matter moved, as water upon a plain table is drawn which way any one part of it is guided by the finger.[23]

This doctrine is basic for all associationist teaching. *Associationism* is the doctrine that we connect things in memory, in thought, and in all mental life simply because they were connected in our original experience with them; and since our first encounters with things are by means of our senses, the associationist maintains that all the complexity of our mental life is reducible to sense impressions. Consequently, there is a material base for all of our thoughts and actions.

Hobbes had, then, outlined an empirical psychology in which sensation was emphasized as the source of our ideas, and had given a sketch of association which served to explain the interconnections between the elements of experience.

The first great follower of Hobbes was Locke, a man who held a great advantage over his mentor as a molder of opinion. Indeed, a primary note in his great work, *An Essay Concerning Human Understanding*, is the rationality of man. While many had looked with disapproval at the materialistic dogmas of "Hobbism," there was great public acceptance of a humane and enlightened social order, the possibility of which was set forth in his discussion of politics and of education, as well as in his psychological studies which aimed to demonstrate the rationality of man and the relation of this rationality to the simpler associative laws of the mind.

Locke agreed with Hobbes that "simple ideas of sensation" are the properties of experience, and not of the objects outside us which excite these ideas. He added, however, that ideas may be either simple or complex, with complex ideas being created in the mind by its ability to combine simple ideas:

> Thus, if to substance be joined the simple idea of a certain dull, whitish colour, with certain degrees of weight, hardness, ductility, and fusibility, we have the idea of lead.[24]

This process applied to all complex thoughts, no matter how remote they seemed from sensory experience:

> Even the *most abstruse* ideas, how remote soever they may seem from sense, or from any operation of our own minds, are yet only such as the understanding frames to itself, by repeating and joining together ideas that it had either from objects of sense, or from its own operations about them.[25]

It remained for later British associationists to lay stress upon and give content to the notions of "repeating" and "joining", which constituted the basis for integration of simple into complex experiences. Also, there was the difficult task of demonstrating how the entire mental life could be reduced to association, and what physical basis existed for mental interconnections. But Locke's lucid exposition of the implications of empiricism, along with his humanitarian (as opposed to Hobbes' materialistic) approach gave his ideas an appealing and challenging quality which greatly contributed to its strength and influence.

Descartes had, in the 17th century, paced with seven-league boots the road from ancient and medieval psychistic explanations of mental events to a mechanistic foundation upon which Hobbes and Locke continued to build. While the rigid materialism of Locke was to be later rejected, the psychology of the 18th century proceeded by a rigorous empirical yet rational approach that is evident in the work of Hume and Hartley. During this time Descartes' contribution to psychology was not acknowledged, and his thoughts regarding mental phenomena were largely rejected based upon specific empirical errors rather than errors in conceptual approach.

The rejection of the specifics of Cartesian physiology had begun in Descartes' own time. Judging from the report of Niels Stensen, there were, by the 1660s, two competing groups of Cartesian physiologists, those who seemed to take the physiology of the *Treatise of Man* as a literal and certain account of the body, and those like Stensen and his teacher Sylvius, ultimately the most influential of the two groups, who saw it only as a working hypothesis.[26]

Other than a difference with particulars of the Cartesian physiology, there was a misunderstanding of the use of models in scientific investigation which led, ultimately, to Claude Bernard's statement in 1872 that the Cartesian physiology was a "physiology of fancy, almost entirely imagined."[27] The problem was one of taking a model as a literal representation of its original domain, an intent that Descartes never had in mind.

Recalling Hall's statement that "the influence of Descartes was felt at first on the broad conceptual level... and only later, and through the work of others, on the level of concrete detail."[28] Hall then notes that there are two important considerations which apply to "the level of concrete detail."

First, there is the work inspired by Descartes on a physical basis of mind. Second, the concept of reflex action supplied a large amount of detail in the work of Pavlov, who, in 1926 wrote:

> The physiologist must thus take his own path, where a trail has already been blazed for him. Three hundred years ago Descartes evolved the idea of the reflex. Starting from the assumption that animals behaved simply as machines, he regarded every activity of the organism as a necessary reaction to some external stimulus, the connection between the stimulus and response being made through a definite nervous path: and this connection, he stated, was the fundamental purpose of the nervous structures in the animal body. This was the basis on which the study of the nervous system was firmly established. In the eighteenth, nineteenth and twentieth centuries the conception of the reflex was used to the full by physiologists. Working at first only on the lower parts of the central nervous system, they came gradually to study more highly developed parts, until quite recently Magnus, continuing the classical investigations of Sherrington upon the spinal reflexes, has succeeded in demonstrating the reflex nature of all the elementary motor activities of the animal organism. Descartes' conception of the reflex was constantly and fruitfully applied in these studies, but its application has stopped short of the cerebral cortex.[29]

Pavlov found in Descartes' work the inspiration to research what he felt had never before been adequately addressed—the physiological basis of psychology.

Pavlov is quite explicit as to why the physiological basis of psychology had, up until his time, never been adequately explored:

> The reason for this is quite simple and clear. These nervous activities have never been regarded from the same point of view as those of other organs, or even other parts of the central nervous system. The activities of the hemispheres have been talked about as some kind of special psychical activity, whose working we feel and apprehend in ourselves, and by analogy suppose to exist in animals. This is an anomaly which has placed the physiologist in an extremely difficult position. On the one hand it would seem that the study of the activities of the cerebral hemispheres, as of the activities of any other part of the organism, should be within the compass of physiology, but on the other hand it happens to have been annexed to psychology.[30]

C. Arthur Ellis, Jr.

What Pavlov proposes next is equally clear: a new science of physiological psychology. Pavlov noted that this was particularly true since psychology during his time had little if any claim to being a science, so Pavlov concluded that physiologists should take the lead in psychology:

> It would be more natural that experimental investigation of the physiological activities of the hemispheres should lay a solid foundation for a future true science of psychology; such a course is more likely to lead to the advancement of this branch of natural science.[31]

Over the next 30 years, psychologists such as B. F. Skinner of Harvard University, working with the ideas of John B. Watson of Johns Hopkins University (an investigator working at the same time as Pavlov), developed an elaborate world view in which the role of psychology was to catalogue the laws that determine causal relations between stimuli and responses. In this "radical behaviorist" view the Cartesian problem of the mind-body dualism is banished—no such interaction is required.

The totality of Descartes' influence upon physiological psychology extends beyond the scope of this work, yet it is the belief of this author that Descartes' primary influence in physiology and physiological psychology lay in his development of a model of man, based upon mechanistic principles.

Subsequent researchers into physiological psychology, the physiological basis of cognition, have had the benefit of advancements in chemistry, electricity, molecular biology, holograms, analogue and binary computers, and artificial intelligence, to set forth different models to replace Descartes' mechanical one.

Nevertheless, his pioneering work provided the means by which a physical investigation of "mind" ensued, which eventually evicted the soul.

Notes to Chapter 5

[1] Thomas S. Hall, introd., Treatise of Man by René Descartes (Cambridge: Harvard Univ. Press, 1972), p. xxvii.

[2] Phillip R. Sloan, "Descartes, the Sceptics, and the Rejection of Vitalism in Seventeenth-Century Physiology," Studies in the History and Philosophy of Science, 8, No. 1 (1977), 6.

[3] Sloan, "Descartes," p. 6.

[4] Sloan, "Descartes," p. 7.

[5] Sloan, "Descartes," pp. 19-20. The quotation from Stensen is taken from his Discours sur l'Anatomie de cerveau in Opera philosophica, ed. V. V. Maar (Copenhagen: Tryde, 1910), II, p. 23.

[6] Sloan, "Descartes," p. 20.

[7] Cornelius van Hoogehlande, Cogitationes, quibus Dei Existentia; item animae spiritalitas . . . nec, non, brevis historia oeconomiae corporis animalis, proponitur, at que mechanice explicatur, 2nd ed. (Leyden: Gelder, 1676; first published Leyden, 1646), pp. 60-61, quoted in translation by Sloan, "Descartes," pp. 21-22.

[8] Hoogehlande, Cogitationes, p. 135, quoted in trans. by Sloan, "Descartes," p. 22.

[9] Sloan, "Descartes," p. 23.

[10] Sloan, "Descartes," p. 23. Sloan maintains that Regis probably transmitted the Cartesian mechanical philosophy to England in the 1650s or even earlier. This is prior to the role of Stensen in the 1670s discussed in an unpublished dissertation by Theodore Brown, "The Mechanical Philosophy and the 'Animal Oeconomy': A Study in the Development of English Physiology in the Seventeenth and Early Eighteenth Century" (Princeton Univ., 1968). A summary of the dissertation may be found in DA, 29 (1968), 2633A. Neither Sloan nor Brown note Kenelm Digby's transmission of the Cartesian

mechanical plan to England (see page 151 of this chapter). For
other accounts of the Cartesian influence in England see:
M. Nicolson, "The Early Stage of Cartesianism in England," Studies
in Philology, 26 (1929), 356-374; J. Saveson, "Descartes' Influence
on John Smith, Cambridge Platonist," J. Hist. Ideas, 20 (1959), 255-
263; S. Lamprecht, "The Role of Descartes in 17th Century England,"
Studies in the History of Ideas, III (1935; rpt. New York: AMS Press,
1970), 181-240; E. Burtt, Metaphysical Foundations of Modern Science
(1952; rpt. New York: Doubleday Anchor Books, 1954), passim;
Marie Boas [Hall], "The Establishment of the Mechanical Philosophy,"
Osiris, 10 (1952), 412-541; Wilbur S. Howell discusses Descartes
and the Port-Royalists in Logic and Rhetoric in England, 1500-
1700 (Princeton: Princeton Univ. Press, 1956), pp. 342-361;
A. C. Crombie discusses Descartes' role in the formulation of optical
ideas that served as background to the invention of the microscope
in Historical Aspects of Microscopy, ed. S. Bradbury and G. L'E.
Turner (Cambridge: W. Heffer and Sons, 1967), pp. 66-86; Laurens
Laudan, "The Clock Metaphor and Probabilism: The Impact of Descartes
on English Methodological Thought, 1650-65," Annals of Science, 22,
No. 2 (1966), 73-104; and Thomas S. Hall, "Descartes' Physiological
Method: Position, Principles, Examples," J. Hist. Biol., 3, No. 1
(1970), 53-79.

[11] See Sloan, "Descartes," pp. 23-29. Regius' 300 page
Fundamenta medicina appeared in 1647 at Utrecht.

[12] Henry Le Roy (Regius), Fundamenta physices (Amsterdam:
Elsevier, 1646), p. 5, quoted in trans. by Sloan, "Descartes," p. 27.

[13] Hall, "Descartes," p. 55.

[14] Hall, "Descartes," p. 79.

[15] Hall, "Descartes," p. 79 quotes in trans. from Principles,
pt. 3, sect. 44 (Adam and Tannery ed. 8:99 and 9:123).

[16] Brown, "The Mechanical Philosophy," DA, 29 (1968), 2633A.

[17] Marjorie Nicolson, "The Early Stage of Cartesianism," p. 358
cites the source of this letter as Rawlinson mss. D 1104.

[18] Dictionary of National Biography, XXVII, p. 39.

[19] Dictionary of Scientific Biography, VI, p. 446. In 1646
Hobbes also prepared a manuscript on optics, and in 1648 he and
Dr. William Petty studied Vesalius, performed dissections and
prepared the diagrams for the optics treatise. Hobbes' work on

optics was published in 1658 as the first half of *de homine*, the second half of which was a summary of his theories of psychology [*Dictionary of National Biography*, XXVII, p. 41].

[20] Thomas Hobbes, Introduction to Leviathan (1651), in *English Works of Thomas Hobbes*, ed. Sir William Molesworth (London: 1839-1845; rpt. Oxford, 1961), Vol. I.

[21] Thomas Hobbes, *Elements of Philosophy* (1651), Part 4, Chap. 25, in *English Works*, Vol. I, p. 409.

[22] Thomas Hobbes, *The Answer of Mr. Hobbes to Sr Will. D'Avenant's Preface Before Gondibert* (1650), in *Critical Essays of the Seventeenth Century*, ed. J. E. Spingarn (1908; rpt. Indiana: Univ. Press, 1957), II, p. 58.

[23] Hobbes, *Leviathan* (London, 1651; rpt. Oxford: Clarendon Press, 1909), part I, chap. III, p. 19.

[24] John Locke, *An Essay Concerning Human Understanding* (1690) ed. J. W. Yolton (London, 1690; 5th ed. rpt. New York, 1961), Vol. I, Bk. II, Chap. XII, p. 6.

[25] Locke, *Essay*, Chap. XII, p. 8.

[26] Stensen, *Discours*, II, pp. 23 ff.

[27] Claude Bernard, *Leçons de pathologie expérimentale . . .* (Paris: Baillière, 1872), p. 481. Trans. by author.

[28] See note this chapter.

[29] I. P. Pavlov, *Conditioned Reflexes: An Investigation of the Physiological Activity of the Cerebral Cortex*, trans. G. V. Anrep (New York: Dover Publications, 1960; rpt. of 1927 trans. published by Oxford Univ. Press), p. 4.

[30] Pavlov, *Conditioned*, p. 3.

[31] Pavlov, *Conditioned*, p. 4.

CONCLUSION

Descartes' greatest contribution to physiological psychology is the development of a mechanical analogue of the human body and nervous system, the basic unit of the latter being the inspiration for Pavlov's research into a phenomenon we now call the reflex arc. The entire subsequent history of physiological psychology has been built upon this foundation.

While the mechanization of the world picture—including the Keplerian model of the planets circling the sun—had begun years before Descartes, the mechanization of man—including the mind of man itself—was the achievement of Descartes.

The mechanical principles embodied in Descartes' scaled theoretical analogue were a radical departure from the psychistic principles involved in earlier models of man, most of which were based upon theological explanations of life phenomena, including belief in a soul.

To the ancient Greeks and the philosophers of the Middle Ages, for example, a model's predictive ability was less important than its ability to incorporate their conception of a deistic cosmology and man's place within it. This continued to be true with some, even into the time of Milton, who, in *Paradise Lost*, dismisses the importance of choosing between the Ptolemaic and Copernican systems on the ground that it is more important to worship and serve God than to pry into the secrets of the universe.

The value of Descarte's mechanical model of man lay in its ability to offer future researchers the opportunity to prove or disprove the assumptions of the model—and innumerable subsequent ones—by putting them through the ordeal of experimentation. Descartes can therefore be credited as being the first to remove the mechanical functions of the body—even the lower-level cognitive functions of cognition—from the realm of the soul and ground them firmly in the soil of empiricism.

Pavlov and Sherrington, two giants of the physical investigation of physiological psychology, acknowledge their indebtedness to Descartes, and it is through their works, as well as the work of those who followed in their footsteps, that Descartes' ideas have had their greatest influence.

WORKS CONSULTED

Primary Sources

Harvey, William. An Anatomical Disquisition on the Motion of the Heart and Blood in Animals. Trans. R. Willis. London, 1690; London: J. M. Dent & Co., 1947.

Hippocrates. The Sacred Disease. Trans. W. H. S. Jones. Vol. II of the Loeb Classical Library, Hippocrates [Select Works]. London: Heinemann, 1923.

Hobbes, Thomas. Leviathan, or the Matter, Form, and Power of a Commonwealth Ecclesiastical and Civil. London, 1651; Oxford: Clarendon Press, 1909.

Locke, John. An Essay Concerning Human Understanding. London, 1690; London: J. M. Dent & Co., 1947.

Lovejoy, Arthur O. The Great Chain of Being: A Study in the History of Ideas. Cambridge: Harvard Univ. Press, 1936.

Montaigne, Michel Eyquem de. Essays. Trans. Charles Cotton. Vol. XXV of Great Books of the Western World. Ed. W. Carew Hazlitt. Chicago: Encyclopedia Britannica, 1952.

Nemesius. On the Nature of Man. Trans. William Telfer. In Cyril of Jerusalem and Nemesius of Emesa. Philadelphia: Westminster Press, 1955.

Pavlov, I. P. Conditioned Reflexes: An Investigation of the Physiological Activity of the Cerebral Cortex. Trans. G. V. Anrep. New York: Dover Publications, 1960; rpt. London: Oxford Univ. Press, 1927.

Peirce, Charles S. Collected Papers of Charles Saunders Peirce. Ed. Charles Hartshorne and Paul Weiss. Cambridge: Harvard Univ. Press, 1931-1935.

Reisch, Gregor. Margarita Philosophica. Freiburg im Breisgau: J. Schott, 1503.

Stensen, Niels. Opera Philosophica. Ed. V. V. Maar. Copenhagen: Tryde, 1910.

Vesalius, Andreas. De humani corporis fabrica. Portions on brain trans. by Charles Singer as Vesalius on the Human Brain. London: Oxford Univesity Press, 1952.

Secondary Sources

Belloni, Luigi. "De la theorie atomistico-mecaniste a l'anatomie
        subtile (de Borelli a Malpighi) et de l'anatomie subtile a
        l'anatomie pathologique (de Malpighi a Morgagni)." Clio
        Medica, 6 (1971), 99-107.

Black, Max. Models and Metaphors. New York: Cornell Univ. Press,
        1962.

Blake, Ralph M., et al. Theories of Scientific Method: The
        Renaissance Through the Nineteenth Century. Seattle: Univ. of
        Washington Press, 1960.

Blizman, James. "Models, Analogies, and Degrees of Certainty in
        Descartes." Modern Schoolman, 50, No. 1 (1972), 1-32; No. 2,
        183-208.

Bown, Christopher Duncan. "Mid-Seventeenth Century English Natural
        Philosophical Thought About the Brain." Senior thesis
        submitted to the History Department of Princeton University,
        n.d.

Brandt, Frithiof. Thomas Hobbe's Mechanical Conception of Nature.
        London: Libraire Hachette, 1928.

Brooks, Chandler M. and Cranefield, P. F., eds. The Historical
        Development of Physiological Thought. New York: Hafner, 1959.

Brown, Theodore M. "Physiology and the Mechanical Philosophy in
        Mid-Seventeenth Century England." Bulletin of the History of
        Medicine, 51, No. 1 (1977), 25-54.

----------. "The Mechanical Philosophy and the 'Animal Oeconomy'--
        A Study in the Development of English Physiology in the
        Seventeenth and Early Eighteenth Century.' DAI, 24 (1968),
        2633A (Princeton University).

Buchdahl, Gerd. "Descartes' Anticipation of a 'Logic of Scientific
        Discovery.'" In Scientific Change: Historical Studies in
        the Intellectual, Social and Technical Conditions for Scien-
        tific Discovery and Technical Invention, From Antiquity to
        the Present (A Symposium in the History of Science). London:
        University of Oxford (Heinemann), 1961.

Burtt, E. A. The Metaphysical Foundations of Modern Physical
        Sciences. New York: Humanities Press, 1952; rpt. New York:
        Anchor Books, 1954.

Campbell, Donald. Arabian Medicine and Its Influence on the Middle Ages. London: Kegan Paul, Trench, Trubner and Co., Ltd., 1926, 2. vols.

Canton, Norman F., and Klein, Peter L. Seventeenth Century Rationalism: Bacon and Descartes. Massachusetts: Blaisdell Publishing Co., 1969.

Carmichael, Leonard. "Robert Whytt: A Contribution to the History of Physiological Psychology." Psychological Review, 34 (1927), 287-304.

Clarke, Edwin, and O'Malley, C. D. The Human Brain and Spinal Cord: A Historical Study Illustrated by Writings from Antiquity to the Twentieth Century. Berkeley: University of California Press, 1968.

Clarke, Edwin, and Dewhurst, Kenneth. An Illustrated History of Brain Function. Berkeley and Los Angeles: University of California Press, 1972.

Crombie, Alistair C. "Descartes." Scientific American, 201, No. 4 (1959), 160-173.

----------. "Some Aspects of Descartes' Attitude Toward Hypothesis and Experiment." Collection des travaux de l'Académie d'Histoire des Sciences, 11 (1960), 192-201.

----------. "The Mechanistic Hypothesis and the Scientific Study of Vision." In Historical Aspects of Microscopy. Eds. Savile Bradbury and G. L'E. Turner. Cambridge, England: W. Heffer for the Royal Microscopical Society, 1967, pp. 66-112.

----------. "Marin Mersenne (1588-1648) and the Seventeenth-Century Problem of Scientific Acceptability." Physis, 17, Nos. 3 and 4 (1975), 186-204.

Diamond, Solomon. "Seventeenth Century French Connectionism: La Forge, D'Illy, and Regis." Journal of the History of the Behavioral Sciences, 5, No. 1 (1969), 3-9.

Dijksterhuis, E. J. The Mechanization of the World Picture. Trans. C. Dikshoorn. Oxford: Clarendon Press, 1961.

Dreyful-Le Foyer, H. "Les conceptions medicales de Descartes." Revue de Metaphysique et de Morale, 44 (1937), 237-286.

Ellenberger, Henri F. The Discovery of the Unconscious: The History and Evolution of Dynamic Psychiatry. New York: Basic Books, 1970.

Fearing, Franklin. Reflex Action. Baltimore: The Williams and Wilkins Co', 1930.

----------. 'René Descartes: A Study in the History of Reflex
    Action.' Psychological Review, 36 (1929), 375-388.

----------. "Jan Swammerdam: A Study in the History of Comparative
    and Physiological Psychology of the 17th Century." American
    Journal of Psychology, 41 (1929), 442-445.

Foster, Sir Michael. Lectures on the History of Physiology During
    the 16th, 17th and 18th Centuries. Cambridge: Cambridge
    University Press, 1901.

Fulton, J. C. Muscular Contraction and Reflex Control of Movement.
    Baltimore: The Willen and Wilkins Co., 1926.

Georges-Berthier, Aug. "Le Mécanisme Cartésien et la physiologie
    au VIIe siècle." Isis, 2 (1914), 37-89; 3 (1920), 21-58.

Gewirtz, Alan. "Experience and the Non-Mathematical in the Cartesian
    Method." Journal of the History of Ideas, 2, No. 1 (1941),
    183-210.

Groot, J. V. de. Het leven van de H. Thomas van Acuino. Utrecht:
    Van Rossum, 1907.

Gruner, O. C. A Treatise on the Canon of Medicine of Avicenna
    Incorporating a Translation of the First Book. London:
    Luzac, 1930.

Hall, G. Stanley. "A Sketch of the History of Reflex Action."
    The American Journal of Psychology, 3, No. 1 (1890), 71-86.

Hall, T. S. "Descartes' Physiological Method: Position, Principles,
    Examples." Journal of the History of Biology, 3, No. 1 (1970),
    53-59.

----------. History of General Physiology. Chicago: University
    of Chicago Press, 1969. 2 vols.

----------. Ideas of Life and Matter (Intro., note 15).

Hall, Thomas S. Ideas of Life and Matter: Studies in the History
    of General Physiology, 600 B.C.-1900 A.D. 2 vols. Chicago:
    Univ. of Chicago Press, 1969.

Hodge, C. F. "A Sketch of the History of Reflex Action." The
    American Journal of Psychology, 3, No. 2 (1890), 149-167.

Hoff, Hebbel E. and Kellaway, Peter. "The Early History of the
    Reflex." Journal of the History of Medicine and Allied
    Sciences, 7 (1952), 211-249.

Huxley, T. H. "On the Hypothesis that Animals are Automata." In
    *Significant Contributions to the History of Psychology, Series
    E: Physiological Psychology, IV.* (1976); rpt. from the *Fort-
    nightly Review*, n.p., 16 (1874), 555-580.

Jaynes, Julian. "The Problem of Animate Motion in the Seventeenth
    Century." *Journal of the History of Ideas*, 31, No. 2 (1970),
    219-234.

Keele, Kenneth D. "Physiology." In *Medicine in the Seventeenth
    Century.* Ed. Allen G. Debus. Berkeley: UCLA Press, 1974,
    pp. 147-181.

King, Lester S. "The Transformation of Galenism." In *Medicine in
    Seventeenth Century England.* Ed. Allen G. Debus. Berkeley:
    UCLA Press, 1974, pp. 7-31.

Koyré, Alexander. "Descartes After Three Hundred Years." *Buffalo
    University Studies*, 19 (1951-1952), 5-37.

La Mettrie, J. O. de. *Oeuvres philosophiques.* The Hague, 1745;
    rpt. Amsterdam, 1753.

Lamprecht, Sterling P. "The Role of Descartes in Seventeenth-
    Century England." In *Studies in the History of Ideas, III.*
    New York: Columbia University Press, 1935. Pp. 181-240.

LeFleur, Laurence J. "Descartes' Role in the History of Science."
    The Scientific Monthly, 71 (1950), 11-14.

Loudan, Laurens. "The Clock Metaphor and Probabilism: The Impact
    of Descartes on English Methodological Thought, 1650-65."
    Annals of Science, 22, No. 2 (1966), 73-104.

Leake, Chauncey. *Some Founders of Physiology.* Washington, D.C.:
    American Physiological Society, 1956.

Lemoine, [Jacques] Albert [Felix]. *L'Ame et le Corps: études de
    philosophie morale et naturelle.* Paris: Didier, 1862.

Lewontin, R. C. "Biological Models," in the *Dictionary of the
    History of Ideas.* New York: Charles Scribner's Sons,
    1973.

Lindeboom, G. A. *Descartes and Medicine.* Amsterdam: Rodopi,
    1978.

Lindroth, Sten. "Harvey, Descartes, and Young Olaus Rudbeck."
    Journal of the History of Medicine and Allied Sciences, 12
    (1957), 208-219.

Magoun, H. W. "Development of Ideas Relating the Mind with the
    Brain." In *The Historical Development of Physiological
    Thought.* Ed. Cranefield and Brooks. New York: Hafner,
    1959, pp. 81-89.

Marban, Eduarco, and Gariepy, Thomas P. "A Thematic Approach to Physiology." The Yale Journal of Biology and Medicine, 51 (1978), 565-570.

McReynolds, Paul. "Statues, Clocks, and Computers: On the History of Models in Psychology." Proceedings of the 79th Annual Convention of the American Psychological Association, 6 (1971), 715-716.

Mesnard, Pierre. "L'Esprit de la Physiologie Cartésienne." Archives de Philosophie, 13, No. 2 (1937), 181-220.

Nicolson, Marjorie. "The Early Stage of Cartesianism in England." Studies in Philology, 23 (1929), 356-374.

O'Malley, C. D. and Saunders, J. B. Leonardo da Vinci on the Human Body. New York: Henry Schuman, 1952.

Pagel, Walter. "Medieval and Renaissance Contributions to Knowledge of the Brain and its Functions." In The History and Philosophy of Knowledge of the Brain and its Functions. Ed. Frederick N. L. Poynter. Illinois: Charles C. Thomas, 1957, pp. 95-113.

Peck, Arthur L. "The Connate Pneuma: An Essential Factor in Aristotle's Solutions to the Problems of Reproduction and Sensation." In Vol. 1 of Science, Medicine, and History: Essays in the Evolution of Scientific Thought and Medical Practice Written in Honour of Charles Singer. Ed. E. Ashworth Underwood. London: Oxford University Press, 1953. Pp. 111-121.

Radner, Daisie. "Descartes' Notion of the Union of Mind and Body." Journal of the History of Philosophy, 9, No. 2 (1971), 159-170.

Rahman, F. Avicenna's Psychology: An English Translation of Kitáb al-Najâb, Book III, Chapter VI, with Historical-Philosophical Notes and Textual Improvements on the Cairo Edition. London: Oxford University Press, 1952.

Randall, J. H. (Jr.). "The Development of the Scientific Method in the School of Padua." Journal of the History of Ideas, I, No. 2 (1940), 177-206.

Rée, Jonathan. Descartes. New York: Pica Press, 1975.

Riese, Walther, and Hoff, Eube C. "A History of the Doctrine of Cerebral Localization: Sources, Anticipations, and Basic Reasoning." Journal of the History of Medicine and Allied Sciences, 5 (1950), 50-71.

----------. "Descartes' Ideas of Brain Function." In The History and Philosophy of Knowledge of the Brain and its Functions. Ed. Frederick N. L. Poynter. Illinois: Charles C. Thomas, 1957. Pp. 115-134.

----------. "An Outline of a History of Ideas in Neurology."
Bulletin of the History of Medicine, 23, No. 2 (1949),
111-136.

Rosenfield, Leonora. From Beast-Machine to Man-Machine: Animal
Soul in French Letters from Descartes to La Mettrie. New
York: Octagon Press, 1968.

Rothschuh, Karl E. History of Physiology. Trans. Guenter B. Risse.
New York: Robert E. Krieger, 1973.

Sarton, George. The Appreciation of Ancient and Medieval Science
During the Renaissance. Philadelphia: University of
Pennsylvania Press, 1955.

Scott, J. F. The Scientific Work of Descartes. London: Taylor and
Francis, n.d.

SeBoyar, Gerald E. "Bartholomaeus Anglicus and His Encyclopaedia."
Journal of English and Germanic Philology, 19 (1920), 168-
189.

Singer, Charles. "Brain Dissection Before Vesalius." Journal of
the History of Medicine and Allied Sciences, 11 (1956), 261-
274.

----------. "Notes on Renaissance Artists and Practical Anatomy."
Journal of the History of Medicine and Allied Sciences,
5 (1950), 155-162.

----------. "Some Galenic and Animal Sources of Vesalius." Journal
of the History of Medicine and Allied Sciences, 1, No. 1
(1946), 6-24.

----------. The Evolution of Anatomy: A Short History of Anatomical
and Physiological Discovery to Harvey. New York: Alfred A.
Knopf, 1925.

Sloan, Phillip R. "Descartes, the Sceptics, and the Rejection of
Vitalism in Seventeenth-Century Physiology." Studies in the
History and Philosophy of Science, 8, No. 1 (1977), 1-28.

Smith, Homer W. "The Biology of Consciousness." In The Historical
Development of Physiological Thought. Ed. Granefield and
Brooks. New York: Hafner, 1959, pp. 109-136.

Sudhoff, Walther. "Die Lehre von den Hirnventrikeln in textlicher
und graphischer Tradition des Altertums und Mittelalters."
Archiv für Geschichte der Medizin, 7, No. 3 (1913), 149-205.

Tellier, Auguste. "Descartes et la Medecine, ou Relations de
     René Descartes avec les Médicins de son temps suivi d'un
     exposé des idées médicales de Descartes." A Thesis submitted
     for the Doctorate in Medicine at the L'École de Médecine,
     Paris (1928).

Temkin, Owsei. Galenism: Rise and Decline of a Medical Philosophy.
     New York: Cornell University Press, 1973.

Thorndike, Lynn. A History of Magic and Experimental Science. New
     York: MacMillan, 1923-58.

Wallace, William A. Causality and Scientific Explanation. Ann
     Arbor: University of Michigan Press, 1974. 2 vols.

Woollam, D. H. M. "Concepts of the Brain and its Functions in
     Classical Antiquity." In The History and Philosophy of
     Knowledge of the Brain and its Functions. Ed. F. N. L. Poynter.
     Illinois: Charles C. Thomas, 1958. Pp. 5-18.

Wright, John P. "Hysteria and Mechanical Man." Journal of the
     History of Ideas, 41, No. 2 (1980), 233-247.

www.ingramcontent.com/pod-product-compliance
Lightning Source LLC
Chambersburg PA
CBHW080050280326

41934CB00014B/3273